PRAISE FOR *We're Monsanto*

"Compelling! *We're Monsanto* exposes Monsanto's true colors. A must-read for anybody who thinks Monsanto is actually saving the world. Bravo!"

— Stephanie Seneff, Ph.D.
Senior Research Scientist at the MIT Computer Science and Artificial Intelligence Laboratory. Coauthor of *Glyphosate's Suppression of Cytochrome P450 Enzymes and Amino Acid Biosynthesis by the Gut Microbiome: Pathways to Modern Diseases.*

"Finally, a writer has chronicled in a comprehensive and readable way, the lies that Monsanto tells the world about its 'products and solutions' while creating immeasurable suffering and despair all over the planet. For anyone with doubts about the role of the biotech industry in destroying lives and life, this book is a must-read."

— Dr. Ann López
Professor, author, and director
Center for Farmworker Families

WE'RE MONSANTO

Feeding the World, Lie After Lie

— Book One —

Chris

Mayorganic
blessings to you on!
Brett

Brett Wilcox

Wilcox Works, LLC

Sitka, Alaska, USA

We're Monsanto
Feeding the World, Lie After Lie
Book One

by Brett Wilcox

Paperback edition, 1st printing
Copyright © 2013 Brett Wilcox

Contact information at www.RunningTheCountry.com

Cover Illustration: Brittany and Brett Wilcox
Text Formatting: Brett Wilcox

ISBN-13: 978-1492312918
ISBN-10: 1492312916

Trademark Acknowledgements:

StarLink® is a registered trademark of Aventis Crop Science. Roundup® and Roundup Ready® are registered trademarks of Monsanto Company.

Coming Soon
by Brett Wilcox

We're Monsanto
Still Feeding the World, Lie After Lie
— Book Two —

Sexy Body Sexy You
Unleash the Secrets to
Weight Loss, Life, Love and Loot

Dedication

Thanks, Dad, for growing and
freely sharing your garden.
We honor your memory.

Acknowledgements

The threat of irresponsible biotechnology through genetic engineering has existed for more than twenty years. I am indebted to the individuals, scientists, and organizations that have raised the warning cry from the beginning and have fought the long and challenging battle against self-serving corporate and governmental interests.

I am grateful to the millions of people around the world who are now marching against Monsanto and other destructive entities.

I extend sincere thanks to the many photographers who freely shared their March Against Monsanto and related photos. Nearly all protest photos were taken on May 25, 2013, the date of the first global March Against Monsanto.

Additional thanks to Prof. Gilles-Eric Séralini and his team of scientists for their research and for sharing their photo of the rat with tumors, and to Mr. Prashant Panjiar for sharing his poignant photos of the families and friends of deceased Indian farmers.

Thanks to my editor, Jim Catano, for his commitment to an equitable world and to better books.

Finally, thanks to the love of my life, Kris, and to our children. Their support and patience helped turn the seed of an idea into a fruit-bearing book.

Monsanto and Company

While Monsanto is the primary focus of this book, due to the global negative impacts of its activities, there are equally important struggles taking place opposing other agribusiness including Syngenta, Bayer, Dow AgroSciences, DuPont Pioneer, and BASF.

We're Monsanto

"We're Monsanto, and we're working with farmers and partners worldwide to realize a vision for sustainable agriculture."

— Monsanto

Contents

Introduction

"I'd like to tell you a story."[1]

So said Hendrik A. Verfaillie, a former Monsanto President and CEO, in a speech titled, "A new Pledge For a New Company," at the Farm Journal Conference in Washington, D.C. in November 2000. He then proceeded to tell the stories of biotechnology and Monsanto.

And what tales he told!

Biotechnology would cause the environment to flourish, improve nutrition, feed the hungry, heal the sick, reduce the need for pesticides, increase yields, benefit wildlife, conserve the soil, retain moisture, and mitigate the effects of drought.

And Monsanto had conducted "thousands of studies" to ensure that the miracle of biotechnology was absolutely safe. Blinded by enthusiasm, Verfaillie said Monsanto had somehow failed to notice that biotechnology raised "major issues for people – issues of ethics, of choice, of trust, even of democracy and globalization."

Never fear. Monsanto was committed to overcoming all obstacles. To that end, they developed a new and improved pledge, to help them fulfill their "promise for sustainable agriculture." This new Monsanto pledge includes the following five elements – dialogue, transparency, respect, sharing and delivering benefits.

Verfaillie concluded his speech with these words: "This is the story we at Monsanto have chosen to tell, and to live. And we welcome you to join us, and be our partners, in living that story." Verfaillie's speech was truly inspiring, but it was largely untrue.

Verfaillie was not the first Monsanto exec to tell stories. The company has been spinning stories for over a century. And like Verfaillie's fictions told in 2000, Monsanto's stories both before and after have been based on lies.

If you are like millions of others throughout the world, you've grown sick and tired (literally) of Monsanto's products, poisons, and lies.

You're ready for the truth, and with dozens of photographs, illustrations, and thoroughly documented text, *We're Monsanto: Feeding the World, Lie After Lie* delivers it.

This book will empower you to say "No!" to the world's most hated company and "Yes!" to a healthier planet free of Monsanto's poisons.

Together we can stop Monsanto. Indeed, we must stop Monsanto before Monsanto stops the world. Such a statement may sound like an exaggeration. Prepare to see the evidence that it is not.

"Worrying about starving future generations won't feed them. Food biotechnology will."
We're Monsanto

Lie #1: Monsanto Will Feed a Hungry World[1]

The problem? Massive population growth and mass starvation.

The solution? Monsanto's biotechnology.

The problem with Monsanto's #1 solution to the world's #1 problem? It's all a lie.

The solution? Don't believe Monsanto.

Dr. Vandana Shiva states that the idea that biotechnology will feed the world's hungry "is on every level a deception. First of all, the kinds of things they're producing don't feed the Third World. ... Soybeans go to feed the pigs and the cattle of the North. ... All the investments in agriculture are about increasing chemical sales and increasing monopoly control ... All this is taking place in the private domain, by corporations that are not in the business of charity. They are in the business of selling. The food they will produce will be even more costly."[2]

From *Rachel's Environment and Health Weekly*, we read, "Neither Monsanto nor any of the other genetic engineering companies appears to be developing genetically engineered crops that might solve global food shortages. Quite the opposite. ... The new genetically engineered seeds ... produce crops largely intended as feed for meat animals, not to provide protein for people. The genetic engineering revolution has nothing to do with feeding the world's hungry."[3]

Monsanto sells their feeding-the-hungry lie with images of poor and hungry people. People of influence from 18 African countries responded to Monsanto's shameful exploitation of poverty and hunger as follows:

"We ... strongly object that the image of the poor and hungry from our countries is being used by giant multinational corporations to push a technology that is neither safe, environmentally friendly, nor economically beneficial to us. We do not believe that such companies or gene technologies will help our farmers to produce the food that is needed. ... On the contrary ... it will undermine our capacity to feed ourselves."[4]

The people in power at Monsanto have always had as their first priority self enrichment, regardless of the resulting destruction. The poor and the hungry serve Monsanto's mission only as heart-rending images—images Monsanto exploits to exploit your fear and compassion, to con you into believing that perhaps, in some distant day, Monsanto will be able to deliver on its promise to feed the world's hungry. But remember this truth: where Monsanto is present, compassion is absent.

So even if Monsanto were able to feed the world's hungry, why would it?

"The Monsanto company works for the world's food producers, delivering products and solutions to help them reach their goals in ways that meet the world's growing food and fiber needs, conserve natural resources and improve the environment."
We're Monsanto

Lie #2: Monsanto Improves the Environment[1]

The dead zone. That's what scientists call the area in the Gulf of Mexico surrounding the mouth of the Mississippi River. When Monsanto—one of the world's major polluters[2]—claims that its "products and solutions" "conserve natural resources and improve the environment," that's called a lie.

Any marketer knows that it's all about emphasizing the good while hiding the bad. But when your primary "products and solutions" are poisons and the effects of those poisons even show up on images from NASA satellites, you've got a lot to hide.

Elizabeth Kucinich, Policy Director with Center for Food Safety writes about Monsanto's contribution to the Gulf of Mexico dead zone. "Monsanto encourages corn-on-corn farming and has even given clinics to entice farmers to drop their beneficial rotations and adopt this extremely bad practice. ...

"Misguided U.S. agricultural policy is driving historically high levels of corn cultivation through massive support for ethanol production. GE corn is facilitating this misguided policy by making it possible to grow corn-on-corn, but only at the cost of rootworm resistance and increased use of toxic chemical insecticides and fungicides. Still worse, more corn means more fertilizers washing into the waterways, which in turn generate an ever-widening dead zone in the Gulf of Mexico."[3]

Rather than claiming to "improve the environment," Monsanto marketers could at least attempt to be honest and use phrasing such as, "mitigate damage," "reduce pollution," "minimize loss of habitat," but in Monsanto's case, even those phrases would be dishonest. This corporation has repeatedly demonstrated that filling its own coffers comes first even if it means filling the environment with poisons.[4]

So what's Monsanto's actual solution? Exchange the word "poisons" with the euphemism "products and solutions." When talking about the environment, use happy words like "conserve" and "improve." And sell people on the idea that Monsanto is feeding and clothing the world. Weave these words in such a way that the public finds itself in a kind of Twilight Zone—a Monsanto Zone, if you will—where a mega-corporation blesses the earth, humanity, and all creation.

And while the masses are "zoned out," Monsanto grows rich while the world's dead zones continue to expand.

"Our farmer customers are always treated with a high level of integrity, respect and transparency, especially during investigations of potential seed patent infringement."
We're Monsanto

Lie #3: Monsanto Respectfully Sues Farmers[1]

According to Monsanto, it always treats its "customer farmers...with a high level of integrity, respect, and transparency, especially during investigations of potential seed patent infringement."[1]

Read what the Center for Food Safety thinks of this monstrous lie.

"After extensive research and numerous interviews with farmers and lawyers, CFS found that Monsanto, the world's leading agricultural biotechnology company, has used heavy-handed investigations and ruthless prosecutions that have fundamentally changed the way many American farmers farm. The result has been nothing less than an assault on the foundations of farming practices and traditions that have endured for centuries in this country and millennia around the world, including one of the oldest, the right to save and replant crop seed. ...

"No farmer is safe from the long reach of Monsanto. Farmers have been sued after their fields were contaminated by pollen or seed from someone else's genetically engineered crop; when genetically engineered seed from a previous year's crop has sprouted, or 'volunteered,' in fields planted with non-genetically engineered varieties the following year; and when they never signed Monsanto's technology agreement but still planted the patented crop seed. In all of these cases, because of the way patent law has been applied, farmers are technically liable. It does not appear to matter if the use was unwitting or a contract was never signed." [2]

Contrast the words "integrity, respect, and transparency" with Chris Parker's description of Monsanto's investigation tactics. "Armed with lawyers and private investigators, the company has embarked on a campaign of spying and intimidation to stop any farmer from replanting seeds.

"Farmers call them the 'seed police,' using words such as 'gestapo' and 'mafia' to describe the company's tactics. Monsanto's agents fan out into small towns, where they secretly videotape and photograph farmers, store owners, and co-ops; infiltrate community meetings; and gather information from informants. Some Monsanto agents pretend to be surveyors; others confront farmers on their land and try to pressure them into signing papers that give Monsanto access to their private records."[3]

"Tom Wiley, a farmer in North Dakota, says it like this: 'Farmers are being sued for having GMOs on their property that they did not buy, do not want, will not use and cannot sell.'"[4]

By the end of 2012, Monsanto had scored over $23.5 million from patent infringement lawsuits against farmers and farm businesses.[4]

One "courteous" Monsanto representative told a farmer who had just settled by paying $100,000 to the company, "We own you—we own anybody that buys our Roundup Ready products."[5]

No doubt, the Monsanto rep said that "with a high level of integrity, respect, and transparency."

"In the hands of farmers, better seeds can help meet the needs of our rapidly growing population, while protecting the earth's natural resources."
We're Monsanto

Roundup
WEED & GRASS KILLER

CONCENTRATE PLUS
MATA MALEZA Y PASTO

- **FastAct** TECHNOLOGY! RESULTS IN 12 HOURS!
- RAINPROOF IN 30 MINUTES!

KILLS

PPN 21208K7-16

Lie #4: Monsanto Has Better Seeds[1]

Yes, better seeds produce more and better food while protecting the earth's natural resources. The lie in this claim—a lie that Monsanto repeats incessantly—is that genetically modified (GM) seeds are better than conventional seeds. What have we learned in the twenty years that farmers have been planting Monsanto GM seeds? Most GM seeds decrease yield and produce nutritionally inferior, Roundup-contaminated food and feed.[2, 3] Those seeds that increase yield do so, not because of their GM traits, but because Monsanto has bought up numerous seed companies, creating a virtual seed monopoly, and then injected toxic genes into selected seed varieties in order to patent their mutant creations.[4] When combined with massive monoculture acreage, Monsanto's Roundup-saturated GM crops wreak havoc on the environment.[5]

Roundup-contaminated lakes and ponds result in frogs producing offspring with malformations of the "skull, face, midline and developing brain, spinal cord." When chickens eat Roundup-contaminated feed, their embryos experience similar malformations even at only one-tenth the maximum residue limit of that for soybeans produced for human consumption.[1] That discomforting fact didn't stop the EPA from raising glyphosate's maximum residue limit yet again in 2013.[6, 7]

And researchers tell us an 81% decline in the numbers of Monarch butterflies coincides with the increased use of Monsanto's Roundup on American crops.[8]

The Union of Concerned Scientists sums up Monsanto's claim of better seeds with the following formula: "More Herbicide + Fewer Butterflies = Better Seeds?"[9]

Of course we know that more herbicide plus fewer butterflies does not equal better seeds.

While Monsanto's Roundup-saturated GM seeds do not protect the earth's natural resources, they do, in fact, protect a valuable Monsanto resource. Let's tweak the Union of Concerned Scientists formula and express it this way:

More Monsanto GM seeds + More Monsanto Poisons + More Monsanto Contaminated Food, Feed, Fiber, Soil, and Water + Malformed Frogs & Chickens + Fewer Butterflies + More Monsanto Lies = More Monsanto Profits.

"On June 19, the World Food Prize named three people, including Monsanto Executive Vice President and Chief Technology Officer Dr. Robert Fraley, as its 2013 Laureates. Dr. Marc Van Montagu and Dr. Mary-Dell Chilton are the other recipients of the prestigious award. All three are being recognized for their individual breakthrough achievements in founding, developing and applying modern agricultural biotechnology to help farmers around the world feed the world."
We're Monsanto

Lie #5: 2013 World Food Prize Recipients Help Feed the World with GMOs[1]

The World Food Prize has been described as the agricultural equivalent to the Nobel Peace Prize. So when Monsanto's Executive Vice President takes the stage with two other scientists known for their biotechnology breakthroughs to receive the World Food Prize, it's a big deal, right?

The U.S. State Department thinks so. "Secretary of State John Kerry delivered the keynote address at a ceremony at the U.S. Department of State" honoring three recipients "for their pioneering efforts and their tremendous contributions to biotechnology and to the fight against hunger and malnutrition."[2, 3]

Kerry's speech read like Monsanto propaganda lifted directly from its website. Among other things Kerry said, "It is simply true that biotechnology has dramatically increased crop yields." Then he went on to describe how biotechnology will feed the world's burgeoning human population.[3]

But what do we discover when we pull the curtain on the U.S. State Department and the World Food Prize?

Monsanto.

Monsanto is so enmeshed with the State Department that Natural Society's Anthony Gucciardi describes the State Department as a Monsanto marketing wing. Using tax dollars, the State Department markets "Monsanto internationally with promotional marketing DVDs and pamphlets."[4]

And Monsanto is one of several sponsors of the World Food Prize. In other words, on June 19, 2013, Monsanto's marketing team leader at the State Department announced that Monsanto gave a Monsanto scientist a Monsanto award for promoting Monsanto biotechnology.[5]

Impressed?

Neither were 81 members of the World Future Council, "a network of global luminaries who 'form a voice for the rights of future generations,' and/or Laureates of the Right Livelihood Award, often called the Alternative Nobel." In a formal statement, this distinguished body said, "In honoring the seed biotechnology industry, this year's World Food Prize—to many, the most prestigious prize in food and agriculture—betrays the award's own mandate to emphasize 'the importance of a nutritious and sustainable food supply for all people.'"[6]

If John Kerry were reading their message, he might say that it is simply true that biotechnology fails at every front. GMOs do not enhance nutritional content, they don't increase yield, but they do grow super weeds, they make farmers dependent on patented seeds and chemical inputs, they increase farmers' dependence on fossil fuels and limited mined minerals, they require excessive water use, and they burden cash-poor farmers with debt. Many of the 270,000 Indian farmers that committed suicide between 1995 and 2012 did so due to crushing debt after they adopted Monsanto's products and poisons.[6]

The World Food Prize is supposedly given to recognize contributors to food "for all people." GMOs don't meet the criteria because most GMOs feed animals, cars (as fuel), or are added to processed and packaged foods, products not accessible to hungry people.[6]

World Food Prize? How about the World Food Control Prize? World Food Domination Prize? World Food Monopoly Prize? World Food Catastrophe Prize? World Disgusting Food Prize? There would be an element of truth in any of those.

If you prize sustainable agriculture, farmers' rights to save and plant seeds, and the right to know what you're eating, then you and your money won't be keeping company with the likes of Monsanto.

"Roundup can be used where kids and pets will play and breaks down into natural material."
We're Monsanto

Lie #6: Roundup Is Safe[1]

Telling the public that Roundup is safe for shrubs is one level of deception. But telling the public that Roundup is safe for kids and pets is beyond despicable. New York's Attorney General took Monsanto to court for this and several other lies it told in direct-to-customer advertisements.[1] The company was fined as a result.[2]

Monsanto made similar outrageous claims in France. They were found guilty of false advertising and fought it all the way to the French Supreme Court which upheld the verdict.[3]

Roundup is registered with the EPA as both a pesticide and herbicide.[4] Pesticides kill animals and herbicides kill plants.

Roundup is poison. And now we know through new scientific research that the complete Roundup formulation is more toxic than glyphosate alone.[5]

The Institute for Responsible Technology lists some seventy references that document the health effects associated with Roundup.[6]

Scientists Anthony Samsel and Stephanie Seneff conducted research that explodes Monsanto's myth that glyphosate is harmless to mammals. The Journal Entropy published their findings in April 2013. The abstract reads: "Glyphosate, the active ingredient in Roundup, is the most popular herbicide used worldwide. The industry asserts it is minimally toxic to humans, but here we argue otherwise. Residues are found in the main foods of the Western diet, comprised primarily of sugar, corn, soy and wheat. Glyphosate's inhibition of cytochrome P450 (CYP) enzymes is an overlooked component of its toxicity to mammals. CYP enzymes play crucial roles in biology, one of which is to detoxify xenobiotics." (Author's note: Xenobiotics are chemical compounds such as drugs, pesticides, or carcinogens that are foreign to a living organism). "Thus, glyphosate enhances the damaging effects of other food borne chemical residues and environmental toxins. Negative impact on the body is insidious and manifests slowly over time as inflammation damages cellular systems throughout the body. Here, we show how interference with CYP enzymes acts synergistically with disruption of the biosynthesis of aromatic amino acids by gut bacteria, as well as impairment in serum sulfate transport. Consequences are most of the diseases and conditions associated with a Western diet, which include gastrointestinal disorders, obesity, diabetes, heart disease, depression, autism, infertility, cancer and Alzheimer's disease. We explain the documented effects of glyphosate and its ability to induce disease, and we show that glyphosate is the 'textbook example' of exogenous semiotic entropy: the disruption of homeostasis by environmental toxins."[7]

Dr. Seneff also discusses her Roundup-related research at length in a video interview with Jeffrey Smith titled, "Monsanto's Roundup Herbicide—Featuring the Darth Vader Chemical."[8]

Darth Vader chemical? Is Smith guilty of hyperbole? Not at all. Monsanto itself promotes Roundup as "The Ultimate Killing Machine." What sort of company would tell you the "Ultimate Killing Machine" is safe for kids and pets?[9] Monsanto!

"India delights as cotton farmers' lives transform for the better."
We're Monsanto

Lie #7: Bt Cotton Improves Indian Farmers' Lives[1]

If you live in India, you've probably had to put up with Monsanto's claim that "India delights as cotton farmers' lives transform for the better."[1]

However, more than 250,000 Indian farmers found Monsanto cotton so "delightful" that they committed suicide—many by drinking Monsanto poison—after being crushed by insurmountable debt caused by Monsanto seed licensing, exorbitant Monsanto seed prices, Monsanto seed monopolies, and decreased yields of Monsanto's genetically engineered Bt cotton.[2]

Indian law states that debt is forgiven upon the death of the debtor.[3] Thus farmers who spend their lives providing for their families accomplish in death what Monsanto had prevented them from accomplishing in life.

Monsanto counters that there are many factors involved in Indian farmer suicides, none of which involve Monsanto.[4]

"An internal advisory by the agricultural ministry of India" cuts through Monsanto's bloody propaganda with this statement: "Cotton farmers are in a deep crisis since shifting to Bt cotton. The spate of farmer suicides in 2011-12 has been particularly severe among Bt cotton farmers."[5]

Dr. Vandana Shiva says, "As Monsanto's profits grow, farmers' debt grows. It is in this systemic sense that Monsanto's seeds are seeds of suicide."[5]

Indians have had enough of Monsanto lies and they're doing something about it. Dr. Shiva reports, "technical experts appointed by the Supreme Court recommended a

10-year moratorium on field trials of all GM food and termination of all ongoing trials of transgenic crops."[5]

How many people from how many different continents and countries will Monsanto kill with its poisons and lies before the world rises up and terminates the terminator?

Until then Monsanto makes a killing by killing ... a legacy that apparently Monsanto and its shareholders continue to find "delightful."

Food　　　　　　　Pesticide

"Existing, approved GM crops are substantially equivalent to conventional counterparts."
We're Monsanto

Lie #8: Substantial Equivalence[1]

The concept of substantial equivalence is the sandy foundation upon which Monsanto builds its genetically modified castles.

GMO educator, Ms. Samm Simpson writes, "When a lie becomes the truth, then the truth becomes a lie. That's the GMO playbook; starting with the 1992 Monsanto led FDA policy of substantial equivalence. ...

"It goes like this: 'The Food and Drug Administration, the U.S. Department of Agriculture and the Environmental Protection Agency have all concluded that food using ingredients from biotechnologically-improved crops is completely safe and no different in any meaningful way from other food.'

"So where is the peer-reviewed research that says it's safe for humans to eat food containing DNA injected with cross species bacteria, such as those resistant to Bt or Roundup or 2,4-D then combined with e coli, a cauliflower promoter virus and topped off with an antibiotic resistance gene? There isn't any."[2]

British researchers Erik Millstone, Eric Brunner, and Sue Mayer addressed "substantial equivalence" in a commentary in the scientific journal *Nature*. "The concept of substantial equivalence has never been properly defined; the degree of difference between a natural food and its GM alternative before its 'substance' ceases to be acceptably 'equivalent' is not defined anywhere, nor has an exact definition been agreed by legislators. It is exactly this vagueness that makes the concept useful to industry but unacceptable to the consumer. ...

"Substantial equivalence is a pseudo-scientific concept because it is a commercial and political judgment masquerading as if it were scientific. It is, moreover, inherently anti-scientific because it was created primarily to provide an excuse for not requiring biochemical or toxicological tests."[3]

Jeffrey Smith tells us that the FDA's own scientists fought the concept of substantial equivalence, and they "repeatedly warned that GM foods can create unpredictable, hard-to-detect side effects, including allergies, toxins, new diseases, and nutritional problems. They urged long-term safety studies, but were ignored."[4]

Decades have passed since FDA scientists originally postulated the potential health risks associated with GMOs. And in those decades we've learned there are indeed substantial differences in the altered foods that the U.S. government tells us are substantially equivalent to natural foods. And these differences have produced a host of serious illnesses and premature death in animal tests.[5]

How then did the substantial equivalence lie get started and why does it continue to form the basis of regulatory policy?

Meet Michael Taylor. Taylor was an outside attorney for both Monsanto and the Food Biotechnology Council before becoming the FDA's Deputy Commissioner for Policy, a position created for him in 1991. "After working at the FDA, he became Monsanto's vice president. The Obama administration has put Taylor back into the FDA as the US Food Safety Czar."[5]

But Taylor is just one pro-biotech player among many others occupying key governmental positions.[6] So it's no surprise that both Monsanto and the U.S. government share the common mission of promoting biotechnology.[5]

Independent scientists know that the concept of substantial equivalence is a sham.[7]

Of course, we must remember that Roundup is applied to most GM crops. The founder of GreenMedInfo, Sayer Ji, reminds us that "Roundup poisoned food is never equivalent to Roundup-free food."[8]

A new study published in the *Journal of Environmental Science and Health* exposes just how great those differences are by linking Roundup to an overgrowth of deadly fungal toxins.[9] Again from Mr. Ji, "Not only would Roundup-ready corn contain residues of highly toxic glyphosate, its 'inactive' yet still highly toxic ingredients (surfactants), and metabolites (AMPA), but it would also be more likely to contain aflatoxins – taken together, represent a veritable nightmare of synergistic toxicities, whose sum harms no regulatory agency yet adequately accounts for."[10]

In summary, Ji writes, "The days of casually classifying the ever-expanding numbers of anti- or non-GMO supporters and activists as alarmists, or GM food itself as 'substantially equivalent' to non-GM food, are over. Those who continue to toe Biotech's party-line, under the much maligned banner of checkbook 'Science,' and in face of clear evidence against its safety, will increasingly be perceived as morally, financially and even legally liable for the damages being caused to exposed populations."[10]

FOOD LABELLING.
IT HAS MONSANTO'S
FULL BACKING.

Before you buy a potato, or any other food, you may want to know whether it's the product of food biotechnology.

Monsanto is a leading biotechnology company. Our potato, corn and soybean seeds are adapted to produce better yields through better control of pests and weeds. In a step on from traditional cross-breeding, a naturally-occurring beneficial gene has been inserted into the plants' genetic make-up.

We have complete confidence that our food crops are as safe and nutritious as the standard alternatives.

Recently you may have noticed a label appearing on some of the food in your supermarket. This is to inform you about the use of biotechnology in food.

Monsanto fully supports UK food manufacturers and retailers in their introduction of these labels. We believe you should be aware of all the facts before making a purchase.

We encourage you to look out for these labels. And, if you'd like to know more, please ask for a leaflet at your supermarket, call our consumer information line on 0800 092 0401, or use our online Comments & Questions form.

(THE INSECT RESISTANT GM POTATO HAS BEEN APPROVED BY GOVERNMENT REGULATORY AGENCIES IN THE US, CANADA, AUSTRALIA, MEXICO, ROUMANIA, AND NEW ZEALAND. POTATOES PRODUCED BY BIOTECHNOLOGY ARE NOT YET AVAILABLE IN THE UK)

To find out what others are saying, call Iceland on 0990 133373 or visit their website at www.iceland.co.uk. Try contacting Friends of the Earth on 0171 865 8222 and at www.foe.co.uk.

Lie #9: Food Labeling Has Monsanto's Full Backing[1, 2]

When it comes to GMO labeling, would it surprise you to know that Monsanto talks out of both sides of its mouth?

Check out these statements from Monsanto's pro-labeling mouth:

- "Food labeling. It has Monsanto's full backing."[1, 2]
- "There's a total misperception that we're against labeling."[3]
- "We believe that products that come from biotechnology are better and that they should be labeled."[4, 5]
- "We believe you should be aware of all the facts before making a purchase."[1]

Now check out Monsanto's anti-labeling statement:

- "We oppose current initiatives to mandate labeling of ingredients developed from GM seeds in the absence of any demonstrated risks."[6]

Monsanto backed its anti-labeling position with millions of dollars to keep GMOs unlabeled in California.

Apparently, Monsanto currently believes that Europeans should enjoy GMO labeling while Americans should shut up and eat their GMOs in the dark.[1]

But that was not always the case. Initially, Monsanto naively believed that Europeans would adore its mutant creations. In those halcyon days, Monsanto actually bragged to Europeans about their wondrous laboratory inventions right on food packages. Then when Monsanto discovered that Europeans hated its GMO's, it suddenly opposed labeling. When Europeans mandated GMO labeling, Monsanto returned to its original position and claimed it supported labeling.[5]

Like everything else, Monsanto's position on labeling is based on profit and public relations.

After Europe mandated labeling, the European GMO market virtually dried up. Europeans taught Monsanto that labeling is bad for Monsanto's bottom line.

It's long past time for Americans to teach Monsanto the same lesson.

Gullible
Mort
Ohno
1976 - 2013
They told me GMOs are safe.
I was gullible.
Now I'm dead.
Are you gullible too?
"There has not been a single substantiated instance of illness or harm associated with GM crops."
We're Monsanto

Lie #10: GMOs Are Safe[1]

If you value your life, the GMOs-are-safe lie is one you best not repeat to the thirty-seven families who lost a loved one due to genetically modified L-tryptophan. That's right. Thirty-seven people died in 1989 when the manufacturer introduced genetically modified L-tryptophan into that dietary supplement. Another 1,500 ended up disabled from the same GM-tainted product.[2]

In 2000, GM Starlink corn snuck into the human food supply, even though it had never been approved for human consumption. People experienced "allergic reactions, some of them severe," to products containing Starlink.[3]

The artificial sweetener aspartame is a genetically modified derivative of E. coli.[4] Yum! "In 1990, more than 5,500 consumers filed complaints to the FDA describing adverse reactions to this sweetener. That accounted for 80 percent of all complaints about a food or additive for the whole year." In addition, a 1996 study linked aspartame to brain cancer.[5] The artificial growth hormone rBGH is yet another genetically modified E. coli derivative. rBGH increases IGF-1 levels in milk. Increased IGF-1 levels are linked to cancer.[6]

Among several other lies involving GMOs, Monsanto told South Africans in 2007 that "no negative reactions have ever been reported." The Advertising Standards Authority disagreed.[7] Trevor Wells quotes the ASA's conclusion: "The statement which the complainant alleges is false, to wit: 'This is one of the most extensively tested and controlled types of food, and no negative reactions have ever been reported.' goes beyond merely indicating safety. It expressly states that out of all the studies done in this field no negative effects have ever been reported."[7]

"Monsanto was ordered to immediately withdraw their claim and given the standard polite warning, which applies to all advertisers, that in future they must make sure that they can substantiate any claims before they publish them."[7] Monsanto stopped running that particular ad in South Africa, but continues to claim on its website: "There has not been a single substantiated instance of illness or harm associated with GM crops."[1] Perhaps Monsanto hides this lie behind the word "substantiated."

With every new study that documents real and substantial dangers associated with GMOs, Monsanto can claim the dangers are unsubstantiated. And rather than encourage scientists to conduct further research, Monsanto reveals its anti-science/pro-profit stance by slandering independent scientists and quoting ridiculous statements such as "there should be tighter controls on experiments performed on animals by anti-biotech campaigners, for the sake of animal welfare."[8]

Not content to simply lie about the harms associated with GMOs, Monsanto and company love to tell the world that—you guessed it—GMOs are actually better and safer than conventional plants and foods. Martina Newell-McGloughlin did exactly that when she told TV physician Dr. Mehmet Oz, "I would probably choose genetically modified foods over other foods to feed to my children, because in fact I know not only are they safer, this is probably the most sustainable production system you can find out there."[9]

Don't expect Monsanto to change its tune any time soon regarding the dangers of GMOs. After all, it still claims Agent Orange "is not the cause of serious long-term health effects."[10] Speaking of Agent Orange, Monsanto and Dow Agrosciences have joined forces and developed a genetically modified corn variety that is designed to resist the toxic effects of both 2,4-D and Roundup.[11] 2,4-D is one of the two main components in Monsanto's horrifying defoliant Agent Orange of Vietnam War infamy.[12]

Food & Water Watch writes, "Corn with 2,4-D resistance could be dangerous to eat because a metabolite of 2,4-D is known to cause skin sores, liver damage and sometimes death in animals. 2,4-D is a potential endocrine disruptor and can affect development. Rats exposed to 2,4-D exhibited depressed thyroid hormone levels, which can affect normal metabolism and brain functioning. Studies found that men who applied 2,4-D had lower sperm counts and more sperm abnormalities than those unexposed to the herbicide."[12]

The Australian Broadcasting Corporation ran an in-depth story on the widespread and decades long use of 2,4-D in Australia. ABC leaves no doubt that 2,4-D and its attendant dioxin contamination sickens and kills the workers who handle it. Those same workers were told that 2,4-D is safe enough to drink.[13]

Agent Orange produced huge profits for Monsanto and Dow while producing ongoing suffering to generations of victims. And if these two chemical giants get their way, "Agent Orange Corn" will soon bomb the environment, the corn industry, the meat industry, and your health.

But don't worry, it's totally safe.

"[Biotechnology] reduces the need for chemical pesticides - with a five percent reduction already achieved in the last five years. That means there are literally millions and millions of pounds of pesticide that have already been eliminated from the environment as a result of farmers using this technology."
We're Monsanto

Lie #11: GMOs Reduce Pesticide Use[1]

You have to give Monsanto credit ... it's a great storyteller. And wouldn't it be wonderful if this particular story were true. But it's not. Non-Monsanto researchers tell another story, and it's a story that exposes Monsanto poisons. One such researcher, Dr. Charles Benbrook, Chief Scientist with The Organic Center, writes, "The basic finding is that compared to pesticide use in the absence of GE crops, farmers applied 318 million more pounds of pesticides over the last 13 years as a result of planting GE seeds."[2] Organic farming champion, Jim Riddle writes, "Washington State researchers have shown that herbicide-resistant crop technology has led to a 527 million pound increase in herbicide use in the U.S. between 1996 and 2011."[3]

Dr. Vandana Shiva told a standing-room only audience in Hawaii in 2013, "The GMOs are not a safe alternative to poisons. They are pushed by the poison industry to increase poison sales and monopolize the seed industry."[4]

More poisons? Is this just more bad news for Monsanto? No! More Monsanto pesticide means more Monsanto profit.

Does this mean Monsanto will stop telling the lie that its GM crops need fewer poisons?

Now *that* would be a story worth listening to!

WE NEED THE BEES! NO GMOs PLEASE

"As a company focused on sustainable agriculture, Monsanto has made significant investments in collaborations and R&D for the betterment of honey bee health, including the formation of Monsanto's Honey Bee Advisory Council."
We're Monsanto

Lie #12: Monsanto Promotes Honey Bee Health[1]

Monsanto asks on its website, "What do Monsanto and honey bees have in common?"[2]

Let's guess!

-Both Monsanto and honeybees play an essential, natural, and beneficial role in the world? Nope! There's nothing essential, natural, or beneficial about Monsanto.

-Both Monsanto and honeybees would be missed if they died out? Nope! No informed person not owning Monsanto stock would miss it. In fact, millions would celebrate.

-Many life forms would become extinct if Monsanto and honeybees did not exist? Wrong again! Many life forms are in danger of becoming extinct due to Monsanto's existence ... including honeybees.[3, 4]

You wouldn't know that if you read and believed Monsanto's webpage propaganda. It paints the company as honeybee saviors, not honeybee terminators. "Monsanto is the leader in the development of new technologies to safely, efficiently and cost-effectively control agriculture pests, predators and diseases. ... Honeybees are the key foundational pollinator of production agriculture, backyard gardens and the environment. Being able to work with the beekeeping industry on honey bee health issues is a tremendous challenge—but one we can address together."[1]

Working with the beekeeping industry? That line's as sweet as honey, but is it really sweet that Monsanto bought Beeologics, a company that existed to protect bees from companies like Monsanto?[3]

Is it really sweet that Monsanto—one of the world's leading bee killers—hosted the first Honey Bee Health Summit in 2013?[5]

How is Monsanto going to help bees? Based on its website, it plans to help bees the way it always has ... with more poisons. Based on a 2013 Time Magazine article, Monsanto is going to help bees by diverting the public's attention from its global poisoning campaign by genetically modifying bee-killing mites.[6]

Sweet! Monsanto's chemical and biological pollutions helped decimate millions of honeybee colonies. So Monsanto is going to solve the problem with more chemical and biological pollution?

Let's answer Monsanto's question: "What do Monsanto and honey bees have in common?"

They both have poisonous stingers. But when honeybees sting, they sacrifice their lives. When Monsanto stings, it risks the lives of virtually every living creature on the earth.

FORECLOSURE
For Sale

"At Monsanto, we are dedicated to
providing farmers the broadest choice
of products and services that will help
them produce more, conserve more
and lead improved lives."
We're Monsanto

Lie #13: Monsanto Improves Farmers' Lives[1]

"At Monsanto, we are dedicated to providing farmers the broadest choice of products and services that will help them produce more, conserve more and lead improved lives."[1]

One sentence. Four lies.

First Lie: Broadest choice of products and services

There are some 20,000 edible plant species.[2] In 1903, U.S. commercial seed houses offered 307 varieties of sweet corn.[3] Monsanto offers only one—Bt corn—a corn variety that's registered with the EPA as a pesticide.[4] Monsanto boasts of offering alfalfa, canola, corn, cotton, sorghum, soybeans, sugarbeets, and if it can beat back public resistance, wheat.[5] These plants offer "two major traits: herbicide resistance and pesticide expression—giving plants the ability to, respectively, withstand regular lashings of particular herbicides and kill bugs with the toxic trait of Bacillus thuringiensis, or Bt."[5] In other words, Monsanto offers only a handful of plants, nearly all modified with the same features. Not much of a choice at all. One hundred years ago, farmers could buy their seeds from numerous different seed companies. Now Monsanto runs a virtual monopoly on U.S. seeds.[6] Prior to Monsanto's biotechnology, farmers could save their seeds for the next season, breed them, resell them, or pass them around to their neighbors. Now? No way! Farmers do, however, have the choice of reporting other farmers for saving Monsanto seeds.[7] Thanks, neighbor!

Second Lie: Produce more

New research from the University of Wisconsin tells the real story. "While some GM varieties delivered small yield gains, others did not. Several even showed lower yields than non-GM counterparts."[5] The families of more than 250,000 dead Indian cotton farmers whose harvests' decreased with GM cotton might laugh at Monsanto's lie of increased production, but losing a family member due to Monsanto's defective crops and lies kind of takes the fun out of things.[8]

Third Lie: Conserve more

As in conserve the environment? This from one of the worst polluters in America?[9]

Fourth Lie: Improve farmers' lives

When GM pollen contaminates non-GM plants, nobody's life is improved. (That's not exactly true. Monsanto profits from Monsanto genetic pollution through bizarre sue-the-victim litigation.[10])

Millions of Monsanto's own customer farmers around the world argue in court that Monsanto isn't the least bit dedicated to improving their lives, but is only dedicated to dominating agriculture, controlling farmers, and increasing its bottom line.[11, 12]

MONSANTO/GOVERNMENT REVOLVING DOOR

"Federal laws carefully prevent conflict-of-interest situations when private sector employees take government jobs."
We're Monsanto

Lie #14: No Revolving Door[1]

The movie *Food, Inc.* makes the claim that Monsanto employees frequently pass through the Monsanto/government "revolving door" to take jobs in key governmental positions. U.S. Supreme Court Justice Clarence Thomas was one such individual. The law firm he worked for represented Monsanto.

Monsanto responds to *Food, Inc.* and the "revolving door" question on its website. To prove that Thomas does not have a Monsanto conflict-of-interest, Monsanto states, "Monsanto was not involved in biotechnology when Judge Thomas' law firm worked for Monsanto."[1] And this from another Monsanto page: "Clarence Thomas worked for Monsanto for a few years but has not been employed by Monsanto since the 1970s, long before the company was involved in biotechnology or owned a seed business."[2]

If Thomas has a conflict-of-interest, it would arise from his relationship with Monsanto people, not from Monsanto products. Monsanto people, not products, fattened Thomas' retirement portfolio.

Monsanto also points out that "the case in question involved a competitor of ours – Pioneer – not Monsanto."[1]

What was Thomas' role in the Pioneer case? OpenSecrets.org provides the answer. "In 2001, [Thomas] authored an important decision in this field, J. E. M. Ag Supply, Inc. v. Pioneer Hi-Bred International, which—while it didn't involve Monsanto—held that new, developed plant breeds are patentable."[3]

Hmmmm. Does *that* sound like a Monsanto conflict of interest to you?

Monsanto's statement also suggests that Thomas would indeed have a conflict-of-interest if the case in question had involved Monsanto.

If that's true then, by Monsanto's logic, Thomas had a conflict-of-interest when he ruled in favor of Monsanto in the 2010 Monsanto v. Geertson case as well as the 2013 Monsanto v Bowman case.[3, 4]

The charge of the "revolving door" might be as weak as Monsanto's defense against the "revolving door" if Judge Thomas were the only person to have walked through it. He's not. Dr. Joseph Mercola lists thirty-five people having zipped through the Monsanto/government revolving door. Mercola writes, "Once you realize just how many of Monsanto's employees have shifted into positions of power within the federal government, it suddenly becomes a lot easier to see how this biotech giant has managed to so successfully undermine common sense."[5]

Monsanto says, "Federal laws carefully prevent conflict-of-interest situations when private sector employees take government jobs."[1] Those laws may have been created with the *intention* of preventing conflict-of-interest situations, but the sheer numbers of Monsanto/government seedy connections prove beyond doubt that neither Monsanto nor the government has any problems with Monsanto/government conflicts of interest.[3]

One final word of defense from Monsanto: "If you still believe we have a revolving door in Washington, you're not alone."[1]

"It's not a secret weeds develop resistance to herbicides. They have for years. Thankfully, there are ways farmers can successfully manage tough-to-control or resistant weeds."

We're Monsanto

Lie #15: GMOs Reduce Herbicide Use[1]

Monsanto claims GMOs result in decreased use of herbicide. We now have more than a decade's worth of data documenting that GM farmers apply far more poisons than non-GM farmers. The USDA's own data documents a whopping 6,504% increase in glyphosate use from 1991 to 2010.[2] Why? Because more and more weeds and insects are developing resistance to Roundup and Bt crops,[3-6] a fact that Monsanto almost brags about on its website.[1]

Why shouldn't it brag? Monsanto's failure to deliver on its promise of decreased herbicide use actually results in more poisons sold and more profit produced.[7] And that toxic fact is something Monsanto tells farmers they should feel thankful for. Thankful is a word many people use in prayer. After reading Monsanto propaganda regarding super weeds and superbugs, perhaps the following is the prayer it expects from Monsanto-dependent farmers:

Oh Divine Monsanto, We thank thee for Omnipotent Roundup. Bless these holy chemicals as we partake of their residue. May they give us strength to spray, we pray. In the blessed names of Monsanto products, poisons, and profits, amen.

Thankfully, there are Roundup resistant farmers who have avoided Monsanto's products, poisons, and lies. May we support them so their number and profit might increase, our health may be preserved, and the earth may be cleansed.

Now, *that's* a prayer that inspires thanks!

"*Comprehensive toxicological studies have demonstrated that glyphosate, the active ingredient in Roundup branded agricultural herbicides, does not cause birth defects or reproductive problems.*"
We're Monsanto

Lie #16: Glyphosate Does Not Cause Birth Defects[1]

Parents thank God when their babies are born with perfect little bodies. Hundreds of Argentine mothers who live near Roundup-saturated fields have given birth to malformed babies, and scientists and doctors believe they need to thank Monsanto. As you might expect, Monsanto denies the Roundup/birth defect connection.[2] It wouldn't bring up the subject at all if it weren't for those pesky Monsanto-independent scientists who link glyphosate to birth defects in laboratory animals and express concern for "human offspring in populations exposed to glyphosate-based herbicides (GBH) in agricultural fields."[3] South Americans who live near Roundup-poisoned cropland experience birth defects at nearly four times the rate prior to the introduction of Roundup.[3] Some have described it as "an epidemic of birth malformations."[1]

Earth Open Source writes that Roundup is linked to "endocrine disruption, damage to DNA, reproductive and developmental toxicity, neurotoxicity, and cancer, as well as birth defects. Many of these effects are found at very low doses, comparable to levels of pesticide residues found in food and the environment." And Monsanto has known or has dismissed this information since the 1980s. Not only that, "the work of independent scientists who have drawn attention to the herbicide's teratogenic effects has been ignored, denigrated, or dismissed."[4]

Yes, scientists have linked Roundup to birth defects. But you don't have to be a scientist to link Monsanto's defective conscience to its insatiable greed.

"The science is solid, and it's world-class. [Monsanto] got the safety studies right. Thousands of studies, receiving some of the most intense regulatory scrutiny ever, clearly established the safety of the products of the new technology."
We're Monsanto

Lie #17: Monsanto Science is Solid[1]

"The science is solid, and it's world-class. [Monsanto] got the safety studies right. Thousands of studies, receiving some of the most intense regulatory scrutiny ever, clearly established the safety of the products of the new technology."[1]

Or so said Hendrik A. Verfaillie, Monsanto's President and Chief Executive Officer in 2000 at the Farm Journal Conference. Numerous other Monsanto storytellers have repeated the same lie since then.

Where are these "thousands of studies?" Only Monsanto knows. If these studies exist, Monsanto has not released them to the public or the scientific community.

JL Domingo writes the following in *Science* magazine: "I suggest to biotechnology companies that they publish results of studies on the safety of GM foods in international peer-reviewed journals. The general population and the scientific community cannot be expected to take it on faith that the results of such studies are favourable. Informed decisions are made on the basis of experimental data, not faith."[2]

Another lie enshrined in Monsanto's Code of Business Conduct reads: "At Monsanto, we know and understand the importance of conducting ethical scientific research. Much of our success depends on building trust with various groups and people, and much of that trust will depend on the accuracy and reliability of the scientific data that we provide."[3]

Tobacco companies used to pay scientists to tell you that cigarettes are safe. Monsanto used to pay scientists to tell you that PCBs and Agent Orange were safe.[4, 5]

Now it pays scientists to tell you that GMOs are safe. Earth Open Source reports that studies funded by biotechnology are more likely to declare GMOs to be safe. We read in their report, *GMO Myths and Truths*, "A review of 94 published studies on health risks and nutritional value of GM crops found that they were much more likely to reach favourable conclusions when the authors were affiliated with the GM industry than when the authors had no industry affiliation. In the studies where there was such a conflict of interest, 100% (41 out of 41) reached a favourable conclusion on GMO safety."[6]

The geneticist Dr. David Suzuki states, "Any politician or scientist who tells you these products are safe is either very stupid or lying. The experiments have simply not been done."[7] The founder of Food Democracy Now!, Dave Murphy, says it this way, "If you think the same company that lied about the health impacts of Agent Orange to the U.S. government and our veterans is telling you the truth about the science behind genetic engineering and the food they are feeding us, you are either a fool, delusional or a member of Congress."[8]

And Jeffrey Smith, the author of *Seeds of Deception: Exposing Industry and Government Lies About the Safety of the Genetically Engineered Foods You're Eating*, uses this catchy phrase when speaking of Monsanto: "They've got bad science down to a science."[9] But isn't it unfair to compare Monsanto to the tobacco industry?

Unfair indeed. People don't eat cigarettes.

March Against Monsanto
Castle Hill, Sitka, Alaska
May 25, 2013

"If the rats don't show any issues from such a diet, it can be assumed a human, who would likely eat foods from this biotech crop as a smaller portion of their diet, would also not have any issues."
We're Monsanto

Lie #18: We Can Assume GMOs Are Safe[1]

What right does Monsanto have to declare what can be assumed about the food you eat and the food you feed your children? For that matter, what right do Monsanto and company have to block, threaten, and intimidate independent scientists from conducting experiments on their products and poisons?[2] What right do they have to omit and distort the raw data from their internal experiments when dealing with the FDA?[3]

If their products are so wonderful, why don't they allow independent scientists to conduct independent studies?[4] Why do they conduct experiments designed to hide the toxicity in their products, experiments that allow them to claim "rats don't show any issues"?[5, 1]

Do you know how many GMO human clinical trials have been published? Not one.[6]

Monsanto is doing everything it can to make sure you're not a GMO science experiment. Let's clarify. Monsanto is doing everything it can to make sure you're not a *real* science experiment, conducted by *real* scientists— scientists who aren't on the Monsanto payroll who haven't already documented frightening illnesses in several animal studies "including infertility, immune problems, accelerated aging, insulin regulation, and changes in major organs and the gastrointestinal system."[6] Monsanto wants you to buy, eat, drink, digest, and absorb its poisons. And it wants you to do it in the dark. Dr. Arpad Pusztai states that Monsanto is doing "as little as possible to get their foods on the market as quickly as possible."[7]

But we are not *completely* in the dark.

We know that the American Academy of Environmental Medicine is right: GM foods cause "adverse health effects" in laboratory animals. Some of these effects include asthma, allergy, and inflammation, altered liver functioning, and changes in the kidney, pancreas and spleen, infertility, and lower birth weight.[8]

We know that the AAEM called on "Physicians to educate their patients, the medical community, and the public to avoid GM (genetically modified) foods when possible and provide educational materials concerning GM foods and health risks."[8]

We know that human health in the U.S.A. has gone down during the same time period that consumption of GM foods and other Monsanto poisons have gone up.[9]

We know that many animals avoid eating GM foods when given the simple choice of GM foods or natural foods.[10]

And we also know there is nothing simple about choosing natural foods while the Monsanto propaganda machine spends millions of dollars to keep GM foods unlabeled.[11]

Monsanto's not a person; it's a multi-billion dollar chemical-spewing ass spreading two-bit lies.

You're worth more than Monsanto's toxic empire. Don't buy its assumptions; don't buy its poisons; and don't buy its lies.

"These [extreme environmental] groups want to 'stop-the-world-and-get-off' and they will abuse and misuse 'science' to achieve their ends. They are avowedly anti-capitalist, anti-development, anti-science, sometimes even anti-farming, and most certainly anti-American, and they want to position America, and its biotech companies, as the 'Great Satan.'" – Phillip Stott

We're Monsanto

Lie #19: GMO Opponents Are Anti-Science[1]

The Monsanto PR team didn't make Phillip Stott's absurd statement, but they liked it so much they posted it on the Monsanto UK website. What's not to like? It expands on the usual Monsanto lie that people opposed to GMOs are anti-science, anti-capitalism, anti-development, anti-farming, and even anti-American.[1]

Wow! That's quite a list!

Anti-capitalism? If capitalism is defined as predatory,[2] unethical,[3] illegal,[4] and lawsuit-driven business practices[5] used to push worldwide chemical and biological pollution[6] onto people that neither want nor need it,[7] then, yes, most people who oppose GMOs would probably say they are anti-capitalism.

Anti-development? If development is defined as biopiracy,[8] the destruction of locally owned farms,[8] mass farmer suicide,[2] and control of the world's food supply,[8] then, yes, most people who oppose GMOs would probably say they are anti-development.

Anti-science? If science is defined as research secrecy,[9] sham experiments designed to support Monsanto's lie that its poisons and GMOs are safe,[10] omitting and altering data,[11] forbidding independent scientists to research Monsanto products,[12] and discrediting non-Monsanto scientists,[10] (sometimes even creating fictional characters to carry out its smear campaigns)[11] then, yes, most people who oppose GMOs would probably say they are anti-science.

Anti-farming? If farming is defined as seed licensing,[12] criminalizing the saving of seed from year to year,[8] lawsuits,[8] vast fields of poison-soaked monocultured GMO crops,[12] genetic pollution,[8] sterile soil,[8] super weeds,[12] super bugs,[12] poisoning pollinators,[12] raising crops that cause "gastrointestinal disorders, reproductive problems, and birth defects," in rats[10] as well as "cancer, hormonal imbalances, birth defects, and neurological illnesses including Parkinson's disease," in humans,[8] then, yes, most people who oppose GMOs would probably say they are anti-farming.

Anti-American? If American is defined as a revolving door between Monsanto and key governmental positions,[13] hoards of lobbyists,[8] bribes,[14] millions of dollars spent "supporting" politicians,[15] inserting "riders" into U.S. laws that make Monsanto immune to governmental oversight,[16, 17] spending millions to spread lies to prevent GMO labeling,[18] controlling the media with money and lawsuits,[19] using the government to pressure and punish GMO-opposing countries,[20] and invading Iraq's agricultural system on the backs of the U.S. military,[21] then, yes, most people who oppose GMOs would probably say they are anti-American.

As for positioning "America, and its biotech companies, as the 'Great Satan,'" people who oppose GMOs did no such thing. Monsanto accomplished that feat all on its own.

"The reason we are in Iraq is to plant the seeds of democracy so they flourish there and spread to the entire region of authoritarianism." – George W. Bush

We're Monsanto

Lie #20: Seeds of Democracy in Iraq[1]

F. William Engdahl is an award-winning geopolitical analyst and best selling author who reports, "When George W. Bush spoke of planting the 'seeds of democracy' few realized he might have had in mind Monsanto seeds."[1]

But Order 81 leaves little doubt. It's one of Paul Bremer's infamous 100 orders imposed upon the newly occupied Iraq. Among other things, Order 81 includes a provision with the heart-warming title of "Plant Variety Protection." Iraqi farmers had been farming their fertile lands for thousands of years, ignorant of the fact that their plants needed protection—protection generously provided by the U.S. military. Enlightened by Order 81, farmers learned that their own seeds and crops were invasive and GM crops were uniform and stable. Who taught them? "According to informed Washington reports, the specific details of Order 81 on plants were written for the US Government by Monsanto Corporation, the world's leading purveyor of GMO seeds and crops."[1]

Ever eager to help feed the world's poor, Monsanto provided its "protected" seeds at subsidized prices. Of course, the seeds came with a contract, stating that farmers were licensed to use the seeds for one season only. They would be prohibited from saving seeds, and if they did so, they would be subject to fines, including loss of farming implements.[1]

Order 81's bizarre connection to the Iraq war makes more sense when we understand Donald Rumsfeld's connection to Monsanto. Prior to serving as Secretary of Defense, Rumsfeld was the CEO of the pharmaceutical company, G.D. Searle.[2] Among other things, Rumsfeld gets credit for pushing aspartame—the dangerous artificial sweeter made from genetically modified E. coli excrement[3]—through the FDA's approval process. Monsanto later bought G.D. Searle and its poopy aspartame in a deal that reportedly increased Rumsfeld's personal net worth by some $12 million.[2]

Dr. Vandana Shiva, a woman who may be America's best friend and Monsanto's worst enemy, offers additional information regarding Iraq's seed bank and unjust wars. "Those wars in Iraq and Iran are not just wars. They are about control over resources. They are about giving contracts. They are about opening up Iraq to the GMO seeds of Monsanto. There was an Iraqi Order 81 that [L. Paul] Bremer passed making it illegal for Iraqi farmers, who are the heart of the source of agriculture, the Mesopotamian Civilization: They could not use and save their own seeds. ... Abu Ghraib, the jail from which all the scandals came, used to be the seed bank of Iraq, and Abu Ghraib the name came from one of their most precious wheat varieties. Now, a changing of a name that was a wheat variety, a place that held the biodiversity heritage of a civilization into a jail for torture, that mutation is what we must understand to understand the deepening violence."[4]

Thanks to Monsanto for its part in liberating Iraq with its seeds of freedom. And thanks to Dr. Shiva for her part in liberating the world from Monsanto lies.

Lie #21: Monsanto Can't Afford to Lose One Dollar of Business[1]

Monsanto tells the world one sort of lie while telling itself another sort of lie. "We can't afford to lose one dollar of business" is the private lie Monsanto power mongers passed among themselves to justify their poisoning of people and the environment with their industrial lubricant/coolant, polychlorinated biphenyls (PCBs).[1]

The irony in this lie is that it's one that Monsanto believes. Of course Monsanto can afford to lose a buck or two to clean up its toxic waste. What Monsanto can't afford is the price it would pay if it fairly compensated every Monsanto victim on the planet.

No earthly sum could pay for the ongoing horrors of Vietnam's Agent Orange victims, or the loss of hundreds of thousands of Indian farmers who trusted Monsanto lies and Monsanto cotton, or the families still grieving the deaths of children to Monsanto's PCBs, or the farmers who have had their farms and finances destroyed by Monsanto's lies, poisons, and law suits.

But beyond that, we are all Monsanto victims. And every day, Monsanto multiplies the crimes it commits against humanity and nature—whether they are crimes in courts, crimes in government chambers, crimes against the environment, or crimes every time one of its genetically altered life forms spreads, infests, pollutes, contaminates, and permanently alters life as we know it.[2]

Monsanto can't possibly afford to pay for it all. And we can't possibly afford to allow Monsanto not to.

"And the truth is that in 1966 when we found out that PCBs were in the environment, we started an investigation journey and we tried to gather information and we acted responsibly."
We're Monsanto

Lie #22: Monsanto Acted Responsibly with PCBs[1]

Lie Detector Alert: Any time Monsanto starts a sentence with "And the truth is," they're likely selling another million-dollar lie ... or billion-dollar lie. And any time Monsanto claims to have "acted responsibly," you can bet your last million dollars that they didn't. A former Monsanto Vice-President, M.A. Pierle, told the same lie using different words responding to an article in Sierra Magazine which had exposed Monsanto's poison and lies to the world.[2] Mr. Pierle wrote, "Monsanto has never concealed any hazard of PCBs" and "claims of cover-ups and sacrificing life itself to corporate profits are untrue and out of touch with Monsanto's way of doing business."[3]

Environmental Working Group tells a different story. "As the company's own documents show, Monsanto went to extraordinary efforts to keep the public in the dark about PCBs, and even manipulated scientific studies by urging scientists to change their conclusions to downplay the risks of PCB exposure."[4] PCBs now contaminate virtually every human being on the planet.[5] Inuit mothers in the Arctic North are warned of the dangers of breastfeeding their children because their milk is toxic with PCBs.[6] Dead whales that wash up on beaches are filled with PCBs.[7] Acted responsibly? If polluting the entire world is acting responsibly, then sure, Monsanto makes, bakes, and takes the toxic cake. Thanks to Monsanto and other PCB polluters, PCBs contaminate much of our food supply.

Organic plant foods offer the best protection against PCB poisoning.[8] In addition to the health benefits you get from eating organic plants, you also get a free bonus benefit: You'll feel great knowing your money supports non-Monsanto agriculture.

If a question ... which you may attribute to ...
nt which you may attribute to ...
o's Medical and Environmental Health Department

e have seen nothing in our preliminary health
r PCB workers or, indeed, in our extensive lon
udies with animals that would indicate that PC
rcinogenic.

Recommendations:

Avoid any comments that suggest liability.
Avoid any medical questions if possible.
Do not offer information on MCS 1238 or our
program. If a question comes up, say our de
was shelved in the late spring when it becan
our proprietary approach would not enable us
with the commodity type alternates being pui
Make NO comments about the U.S. law suits tl
recently publicized.
Make no comments on the PCBs in mothers' mil
have been circulating in the U.S. press.
Feel free to use any of the information cont
attached U.S. press release but avoid liftin
of context.

We're Monsanto

Prepared by: D. R. BISH
                 and D. WOO

Lie #23: Monsanto is Not Liable[1]

When Monsanto was finally forced to shut down PCB production in Europe, it issued a letter which told its employees what to say and what not to say when dealing with the press.[1] "If a question comes up about carcinogenicity, use the following statement which you may attribute to George Roush, M.D., Director of Monsanto's Medical and Environmental health Department: We have seen nothing in our preliminary health studies with our PCB workers, or indeed, in our extensive long-term feeding studies with animals that would indicate that PCBs are carcinogenic."[1]

Do you think Dr. Roush got a special bonus—blood money, if you will—for that whopper?

The authors of this internal memo went on to issue a few "General Recommendations" to Monsanto talking heads such as, "Avoid any comments that suggest liability."[1] Hmmm. When you work for a company that is, in fact, liable for PCB pollution, would this advice have made Monsanto personnel uncomfortable or is lying about liability simply business as usual at Monsanto?

But there's more.

"Avoid any medical questions if possible. ... Make NO comments about the U.S. lawsuits that have been recently publicized. Make no comments on the PCBs in mothers' milk stories that have been circulating in the U.S. press."[1]

In summary, how did Monsanto deal with annoyances like PCB-related cancer some forty years ago?

1. Cite authority, in this case a doctor employed by Monsanto

2. Deny liability

3. Don't talk about it

Fast-forward forty years. Stephanie Seneff, PhD, a Senior Research Scientist at MIT, links the following annoyances to glyphosate: "autism ... gastrointestinal issues such as inflammatory bowel disease, chronic diarrhea, colitis and Crohn's disease, obesity, cardiovascular disease, depression, cancer, cachexia, Alzheimer's disease, Parkinson's disease, multiple sclerosis, and ALS, among others."[2]

How does Monsanto deal with this sort of troubling information?

1. Cite authority: doctors, scientists, USDA, FDA, nearly all of which have financial and personal relationships with Monsanto

2. Deny liability

3. Don't talk about it

4. Threaten, intimidate, and/or smear the researchers who dare suggest that Roundup and GMOs are dangerous.

Monsanto has added a few tricks over the years, but in the end it is fully liable for its bag of lies and fully responsible for the products and poisons it lies about.

Bag Monsanto. Bag the poisons. Bag the lies.

"To date, no commercialized biotech products have ever been associated with an actual hazard to humans or animals."
We're Monsanto

Lie #24: GMOs Are Safe for Animals[1]

Monsanto cites its own 42-day broiler study on chickens and its own 90-day study on rats to prove that GMOs are safe for animals and therefore safe for humans.[1]

The American Academy of Environmental Medicine was not impressed with Monsanto's short-term studies writing, "Several animal studies indicate serious health risks associated with GM food consumption including infertility, immune dysregulation, accelerated aging, dysregulation of genes associated with cholesterol synthesis, insulin regulation, cell signaling, and protein formation, and changes in the liver, kidney, spleen and gastrointestinal system."[2]

Jeffrey Smith writes of one such animal study: "By the third generation, most GM soy-fed hamsters lost the ability to have babies. They also suffered slower growth, and a high mortality rate among the pups."[3]

Rodents—creatures not generally known for their sophisticated palettes—refused to eat Calgene's FlavSavr GM tomatoes. Biotech scientists—creatures not generally known for their sophisticated ethics—forced the rebellious rats to eat the stuff "through gastric tubes and stomach washes. Several developed stomach lesions; seven of forty died within two weeks."[4]

And outside the laboratory, real farmers on working farms in several countries report their animals experience a host of medical problems caused by GM feed. These include low conception rates, false pregnancies, sterility, and a whole lot of dead animals compliments of genetically modified corn or cotton plants.[5]

Consider this: When given a choice between natural foods and genetically modified foods, "cows, pigs, geese, elk, deer, raccoons, mice, rats, squirrels, chicken, and buffalo" refuse to eat genetically modified foods.[6] Remember, these GM foods are the foods Monsanto tells us are "substantially equivalent" to natural foods.[6] These foods are the foods the FDA determined were Generally Recognized As Safe (GRAS) even though the FDA's own scientists knew they weren't safe.[7]

Monsanto also tells us there's no need for human feeding studies.[8] Agreed ... sort of. There would be no need for human feeding studies if society were educated enough to avoid GM foods. But since it is not, and since GMOs will always exist now that Monsanto has irrevocably contaminated the world with its genetic pollution, the studies need to be done. But you don't need to wait decades for the results.

Creatures far more intelligent than Monsanto scientists have already conducted their own studies. Their conclusion?

Forget about "generally" recognized as safe. Animals don't even generally recognize GMOs as food.

KAUA'I, OUR KULEANA

What We Love We Will Protect

KNOW THE FACTS ABOUT THE AGROCHEMICAL INDUSTRY.

Throughout our community, people are asking about the activities of Dow, Syngenta, Pioneer DuPont and BASF — the global agrochemical GMO industry — on our island. We want to know the truth about how they are using our island. That is why families, farmers, doctors, nurses and teachers support Bill #2491.

WHAT WE DO KNOW.

1. These are global corporations. Their goal is to maximize profits. They choose locations with lax laws and regulations. Their CEOs and major shareholders do not live here. Corporate profits do not stay on island.

2. These corporations spray approximately 18 tons of concentrated Restricted-Use Pesticides (RUPs) annually. Pioneer alone sprays pesticides almost 70% of all days, and on each of these days sprays an average of 10-16 times. We do not know how often the other companies are spraying because we do not have a Right to Know.

   RUPs are "restricted" because they have potential health effects like asthma, allergies, birth defects, paralysis, low sperm count, seizures, cancer, Parkinsons and childhood development disorders. Some RUPs contaminate ground water.

3. There is abundant, documented evidence of pesticide drift from agrochemical operations into surrounding communities. 15,000 acres of west Kaua'i GMO land are drenched in RUPs almost daily.

4. Atrazine, chlorpyrifos and bifenthrin have been detected in the drinking water or air at Waimea Canyon Middle School. Chlorpyrifos is extremely dangerous to children, at any level. No tests have been conducted to see if other RUPs used by these corporations are showing up in schools.

6. Many of their operations and test fields are research facilities. They are not farms.

7. Some of the RUPs being used are "experimental" or used with experimental GMO crops. They are not approved for the market because their health and environmental impacts are unknown. We cannot know more because we do not have a Right to Know.

8. We allow them to use their chemicals in non-transparent ways which are not allowed in other places. Local counties and nations have banned many of their chemicals. Syngenta's home country, Switzerland, has restricted many of their chemicals and all of their GMO crops.

9. If agrochemical companies really practiced "Safety First" as they claim, they should agree to a temporary moratorium on new GMO planting until We The People have independent research showing that their practices have no significant impact to our health, land, water and ecosystems.

10. The US Government Accountability Office (GAO) found that the EPA cannot effectively enforce laws related to pesticides.

11. As we have learned from DDT, Agent Orange, and the tragedies of many other pesticides, it takes a generation before we understand the full impacts of our actions.

* Know Your Facts. See www.StopPoisoningParadise.org.

As the EPA has recommended, people should reduce their exposure to pesticides as much as possible. But this is impossible when the chemical corporations operating in our backyard won't even provide us with the most basic of information so we can protect our health.

That's what Bill #2491 is about — OUR RIGHT TO KNOW.

We need to make decisions based on good information and science, not the industry's hollow claims of being "good stewards." This is our land, our future, our health and the health of many keiki to come.

WE ARE IN THIS TOGETHER.

For more facts go to www.StopPoisoningParadise.org.

KEKAHA — agrochemical-GMO
POIPU — agrochemical-GMO
LIHUE — agrochemical-GMO — WILCOX
WAIMEA — agrochemical-GMO
MAHAULEPU — agrochemical-GMO
PUHI — agrochemical-GMO

"Everything that we have seen leads us to believe that this is truly a remarkable technology, with truly remarkable benefits for growers and consumers, for food processors and suppliers, for developed and developing nations, for the well fed, and for the hungry. And this is not a theoretical case for benefits - the benefits are happening right now. They are real."
We're Monsanto

Lie #25: GMOs Provide Truly Remarkable Benefits[1]

According to Hendrik A. Verfaillie, Monsanto's President and Chief Executive Officer in 2000, GMOs offer "real" and "right now" benefits to everyone on Earth—from growers to consumers, processors, suppliers, developed and developing nations, well fed, and the hungry.[1]

Well, one thing is sure. Genetically modified foods provide "truly remarkable benefits" ... to Monsanto. Those benefits include obscene profits, a Monsanto-dominated U.S. government, and the company's dangerous control over the world's food supply. But benefits to you and your family? Give me a frankenfood break!

Andrew Kimbrell, the author of the book, *Your Right to Know*,[2] states, "No one gets up in the morning saying I want to go buy a genetically engineered food. ... They offer no benefits, no more nutrition, no more flavor, no nothing. They only offer risks."[3]

Kimbrell's right. No one in the history of the world has ever gone to the store to pick up another bottle of genetically modified canola oil. No one in the history of the world has ever chosen a restaurant because it serves genetically modified French fries. No one in the history of the world eats GMOs for health.

No one! Nowhere! Never!

But as the Executive Director of Center for Food Safety, Kimbrell is no friend to Monsanto and gang. Is it possible his anti-GMO bias blinds him to its consumer benefits?

What would a pro-biotech man say about the consumer benefits of GMOs? Dale Adolphe of the Canadian Seed Growers Association is absolutely pro-biotech. He recognized in 2002 that GM foods offer zero benefits to consumers, and he tied consumer rejection to the lack of consumer benefits. "If we can get a consumer benefit in there, maybe that will shift the consumers to accept the science."[4]

Nice try, Adolphe, but more than a decade has past and GMOs still offer zero consumer benefits, and, more than ever, consumers reject GMOs *because* of the science, not in spite of it.

But neither Kimbrell nor Adolphe mention one humungous benefit of GM foods: When you say no to GMOs, you receive the deeply satisfying benefit of keeping money out of the hands of biotech bullies and their investors!

Now *that's* a benefit! And unlike Verfaillie's genetically engineered benefit baloney, saying no to GMOs is a very real benefit that millions of people are enjoying, and it's happening right now!

"Recently, there have been many wild accusations about us, with no basis in truth. Our fields have been threatened with destruction, we've been individually targeted and harassed, and our friends and neighbors attacked with hate language and racial slurs. This irresponsible and violent behavior generates needless fear and divides our community. It's not pono."

We're Monsanto

Lie #26: Hawaiians Who Oppose Monsanto and Gang Are Not Pono[1]

Monsanto ran a half page ad in the Maui News on April 14, 2013, in which it portrayed itself as the victim of the Hawaiians who oppose it.[1] On April 16, The Facebook group Save Hawaii From Monsanto described the ad as a "ridiculous, hilarious and pathetic attempt to get some public sympathy."[2]

As Hawaii's current number one bully, Monsanto needs no sympathy.

Waging Nonviolence posted an article four days before Monsanto ran its pathetic propaganda piece. The author of the article, Imani Altemus-Williams, writes, "The island chain's climate and abundant natural resources have lured five of the world's largest biotech chemical corporations: Monsanto, Syngenta, Dow AgroSciences, DuPont Pioneer and BASF ... . The presence of Monsanto and the other chemical corporations is eerily reminiscent of the business interests that led to the overthrow of the Hawaiian Kingdom."[3] Together, these worldwide polluters have invaded Hawaiian governmental chambers, universities, and fields, performing "over 5,000 open-field-test experiments of pesticide-resistant crops on an estimated 40,000 to 60,000 acres of Hawaiian land without any disclosure." In addition, these chemical giants "have sprayed over 70 different chemicals during field tests of genetically engineered crops, more chemical testing than in any other place in the world."[3]

Working with the University of Hawaii and the Hawaii Agriculture Research Center, Monsanto genetically altered the Hawaiian staple plant taro from which poi is made. "'It felt like we were being violated by the scientific community,' wrote (Walter) Ritte in Facing Hawaii's Future. 'For the Hawaiian community, taro is not just a plant. It's a family member. It's our common ancestor 'Haloa. ... They weren't satisfied with just taking our land; now they wanted to take our mana, our spirit too.'

"The public outcry eventually drove the university to drop its patents."[3]

Monsanto appeals to the Hawaiian concept of *pono* in its "ridiculous, hilarious and pathetic" ad. There is no direct English translation for the word *pono*. The Hula Master Pattye Kealohalani Wright describes the traits of a person who is *pono*. Some of these traits include:

- "perfect alignment and balance with all things in life"
- "perfect relationship with the creative energy of the universe"
- "complete harmony and alignment with your custodial relationship with the earth" and
- "caretaker of the land."[4]

It is offensive that Monsanto—a company that routinely violates Hawaii and her people—would dare use the word *pono*, because whatever Monsanto is, Monsanto isn't *pono*.

"The world has largely embraced agricultural technology."
We're Monsanto

Lie #27: The World Has Largely Embraced GMOs[1]

On May 25, 2013, more than two million people in more than 50 countries and 400 locations, assembled in what has been called the largest global protest in the history of the planet.[2]

What did they protest? Monsanto and all that Monsanto symbolizes with its century long legacy of pollution, corruption, and lies.

The Gateway Green Alliance of Saint Louis, Missouri, (Monsanto's headquarters) writes, "Dubbed the greatest protest in the history of the world, the largest of its kind and a grassroots movement that can not be stopped, the March Against Monsanto event that took place on May 25, 2013 all over the world was a success, and the beginning to much more that is going to be the change this country and this world needs."[2]

On October 12, 2013, the people of the world marched against Monsanto yet again. They flood the Internet with anti-Monsanto sentiment. Monsanto-related Google searches list millions of sites that stand as testaments against the corporation.

Following is but a small sample of titles demonstrating unequivocal rejection of Monsanto and biotechnology. These articles were published within a two-week time period:

- "Two million protesters attend 'March Against Monsanto' in 436 cities in 52 countries"[3]
- "Europe, Nations Around The World Rejecting Monsanto"[4]
- "Bullsh*t walks, and it carries an anti-Monsanto sign"[5]

- "UK Organisations Challenge Basis for GM Wheat Trials"[6]
- "Washington farmers sue Monsanto over GMO wheat"[7]
- "Scientists Find Holes in Monsanto GM Wheat Denial"[8]
- "Farmers sue Monsanto over genetically modified wheat"[9]
- "Stephen Colbert On Monsanto: GMO Wheat Is 'The Return Of The Walking Bread'"[10]
- "Massive Database of GMO Evidence gives Worldwide Picture of Harm"[11]
- "Connecticut Celebrates GMO Labeling Victory"[12]

For Monsanto to make the claim, "The world has largely embraced agricultural technology," in the face of worldwide rejection of Monsanto and biotechnology, one might conclude that it is suffering from a severe form of mental illness, schizophrenia perhaps.

Mental illness, yes, but schizophrenia, no. Monsanto is not suffering from delusions or hallucinations. In fact, it is not suffering at all. This corporate monster delights in its global empire, while the people it oppresses suffer.

The DSM-5 lists several criteria for a condition known as Antisocial Personality Disorder. (Author's note: In the DSM-5, "antisocial" means criminal, not shy or reserved.) Read the following criteria and you'll discover that Monsanto and Antisocial Personality Disorder are nearly synonymous terms: Ego-centrism, self-esteem derived from personal gain, power, or pleasure, goal-setting based on personal gratification, absence of prosocial internal standards associated with failure to conform to lawful or culturally normative ethical behavior, lack of concern for feelings, needs, or suffering of others, lack of remorse after hurting or mistreating another, incapacity for mutually intimate relationships, as exploitation is a primary means of relating to others, including by deceit and coercion, use of dominance or intimidation to control others, manipulativeness, deceitfulness, dishonesty and fraudulence, misrepresentation of self, embellishment or fabrication when relating events, callousness, lack of concern for feelings or problems of others, lack of guilt or remorse about the negative or harmful effects of one's actions on others, aggression, sadism, hostility, persistent or frequent angry feelings, anger or irritability in response to minor slights and insults, mean, nasty, or vengeful behavior, irresponsibility, disregard for—and failure to honor—financial and other obligations or commitments, lack of respect for—and lack of follow through on—agreements and promises, and impulsivity.[13]

People with Antisocial Personality Disorder wreak havoc everywhere they go. They often spend their lives in prison. Why should the people who run Monsanto spend their lives anywhere else?

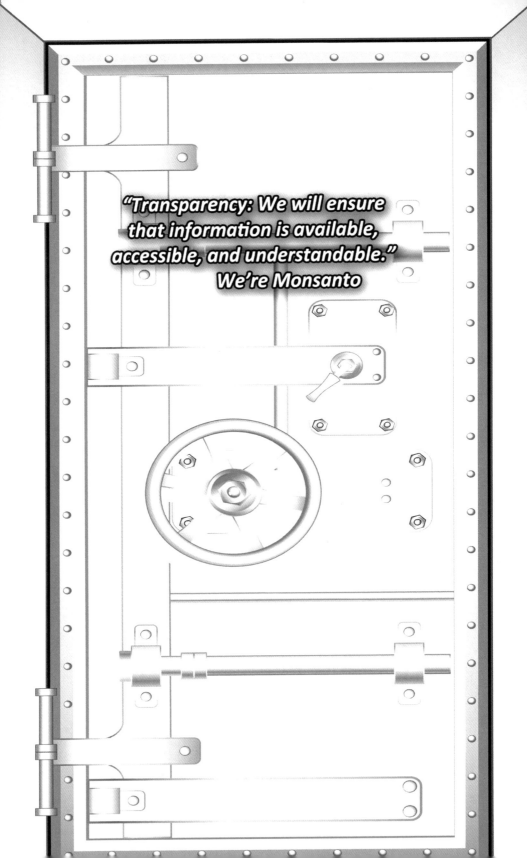

Lie #28: Monsanto is Transparent[1]

Yes, Monsanto is transparent with information ... if it's information that will increase Monsanto's profits. If not? The claim of transparency is just another Monsanto lie.

When asked why Monsanto failed to disclose its failed GM corn field trial results in Denmark, Brandon Mitchener, Public Affairs Lead for Monsanto in Europe and Middle East, said, "I cannot believe that any company would ever voluntarily disclose information that might be useful to its competitors. It's unrealistic, even surreal, that anyone would expect us to."[2]

So much for transparency! To what lengths will Monsanto go to ensure that information *isn't* "available, accessible, and understandable"?

Jeffrey Smith, the author of *Seeds of Deception*, provides multiple answers to that question including: bribes, legal threats that resulted in the cancellation of a TV news series about rBGH, the cancellation of a book critical of Monsanto, the shredding of 14,000 issues of a magazine dedicated to exposing Monsanto, pressuring major newspapers to withdraw stories critical of rBGH, bogus research designed *not* to find problems with Monsanto products, omitting research data, lying about increased GM crop yields, and claiming PCBs, DDT, and Agent Orange are safe.[3]

Does that sound transparent to you? Neither did it to an Alabama court after learning that Monsanto withheld evidence regarding the safety of its PCBs and continued to poison the residents of Anniston. The "court found Monsanto guilty of negligence, wantonness, suppression of the truth, nuisance, trespass, and outrage. Outrage, according to Alabama law, usually requires conduct 'so outrageous in character and extreme in degree as to go beyond all possible bounds of decency so as to be regarded as atrocious and utterly intolerable in civilized society.'"[3]

Outrage indeed!

Adam Eidinger, "an organic food activist and Monsanto shareholder," is also fed up with Monsanto's false claims of transparency. He "organized a march from NY to Washington DC on behalf of honest food labeling in 2011," and he has presented a resolution in two of Monsanto's annual shareholder meetings. He used a hidden camera to record his presentation. Why hidden? Because Monsanto forbids cameras in the meeting. How's that for transparency! He told Monsanto CEO Hugh Grant and some thousand shareholders that the public is fed up with Monsanto's poison and lies. And if it doesn't clean up its act and become more transparent, Monsanto will meet its demise.[4]

We can only hope! Until that day, the only transparent thing about Monsanto is their lies!

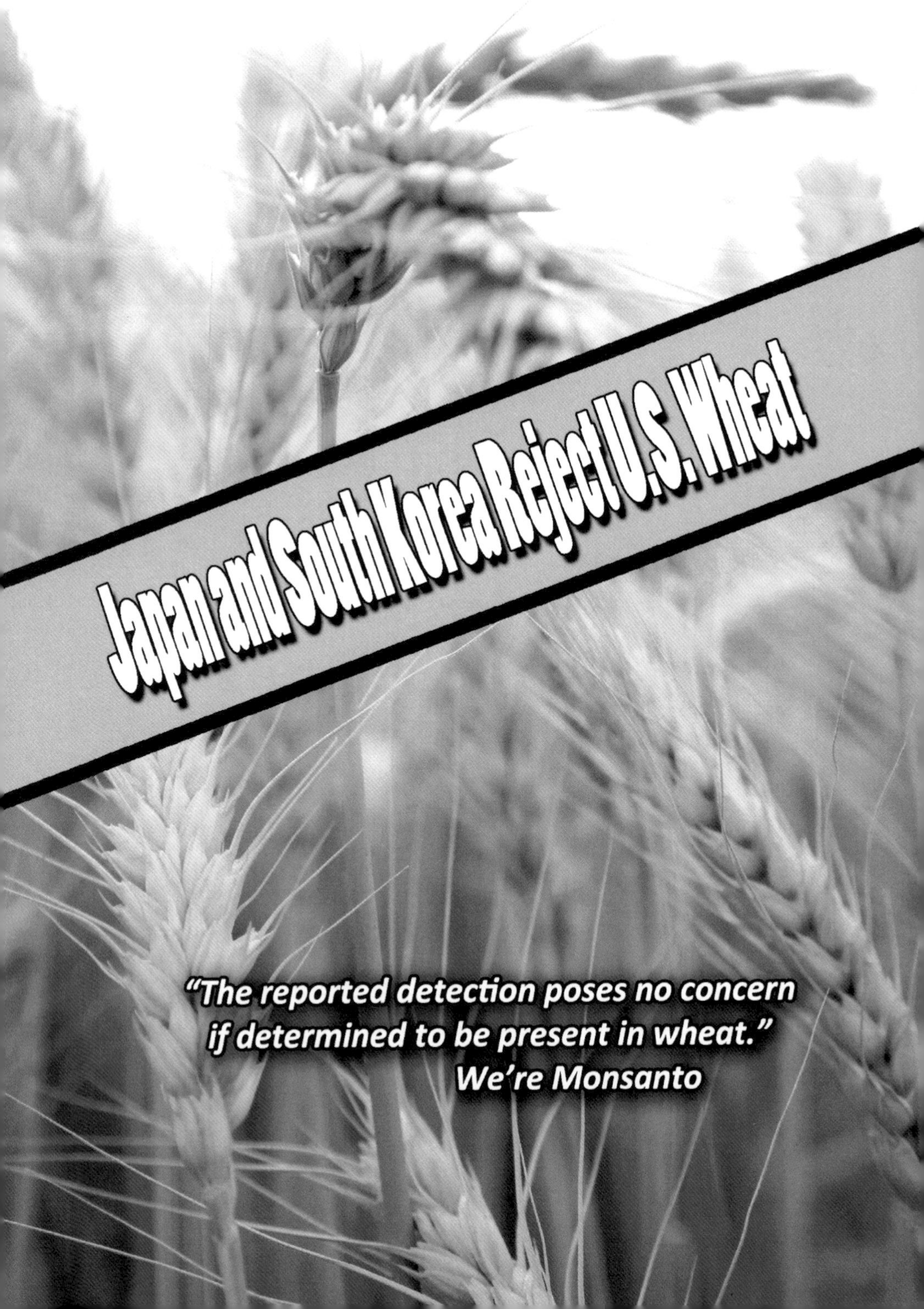
Japan and South Korea Reject U.S. Wheat
"The reported detection poses no concern if determined to be present in wheat."
We're Monsanto

Lie #29: GM Wheat Poses No Concern[1]

U.S. wheat farmers are holding Monsanto responsible for creating and patenting a product so toxic to farmers' financial health that its mere presence on a single U.S. farm resulted in the international rejection and consequent decreased value of all wheat from every farm in the U.S.A.[2] What product could possibly produce such devastating financial losses? Monsanto's Roundup resistant, genetically modified wheat.

Naturally, Monsanto sees itself as a double victim, a victim first to villainous souls that may have intentionally planted Monsanto patented wheat to "sabotage" Monsanto, and second to "tractor-chasing lawyers" that filed suit against Monsanto.[2, 3] Hey, Monsanto is usually the one doing the suing.

There's a frightening irony in the fact that Monsanto created genetically modified wheat with the intent of selling it to farmers, but after that same wheat shows up in a farmer's field, Monsanto suggests that saboteurs are out to destroy it. There's more irony still in its use of the phrase "tractor-chasing lawyers" to divert attention from farmers who seek legitimate compensation due to financial losses they experienced and will continue to experience from Monsanto's unwanted and unapproved transgenic wheat.

This isn't the first time farmers have had to unjustly bear the costs of irresponsible biotechnology giants. "The 2000 release of Aventis SA's StarLink corn cost as much as $288 million in lost revenue and a yearlong drop in the grain's price, according to a 2008 report by the

Government Accountability Office. The 2006 release of Bayer AG's Liberty Link rice cost as much as $1.29 billion in lost exports, food recalls and other expenses, the GAO said, citing an environmental advocacy group. Bayer in 2011 agreed to pay $750 million to about 11,000 U.S. rice farmers who sued the company."[4]

In light of Monsanto's allegation of potential "sabotage" in the case of its genetically modified wheat, one has to wonder how it came up with such an idea. Do Monsanto investigators spread Monsanto seeds while trespassing on farmers' property? Do Monsanto investigators get paid on commission? Do they earn a percentage on court victories?

There's more irony in the fact that while Monsanto claims no responsibility for its wheat found in Oregon, it is currently conducting open-field GM wheat testing in Hawaii and North Dakota.[5]

Of course that means Monsanto is actively planning to unleash yet another version or versions of GM wheat— wheat that will once again result in lost market share for U.S. farmers.[6] And Monsanto will do it with the blessing of the USDA. Considering the fact that the USDA's mission includes promoting American agriculture, isn't it ironic the agency continues to approve genetically modified crops that destroy American agriculture?

Virtually no one wants biotech seeds or food, and absolutely no one needs biotech seeds or foods, but Monsanto doesn't care what people want or need. It will use any and all methods to muscle and money its way into governments, fields, and foods.

Monsanto has always used patented seeds to its legal and financial advantage while shirking responsibility for the immense damage that results from those products.

It's long past time for Monsanto to stop profiting from genetic contamination. It's time for Monsanto to pay in full for the devastating losses farmers experience due to Monsanto's unwanted and—in the case of wheat—illegal genetically modified products.

Bravo to the farmers and organizations that are holding Monsanto's genetically modified butt to the legal fire. But don't expect this corporation to give up on its plans to cram GM wheat down the throats of the world. Monsanto is continuing its global cram-job even after five million Brazilian farmers sued it and "a Brazilian judge ruled in favor of the farmers, ordering Monsanto to return royalties paid since 2004 or a minimum of $2 billion."[7]

After so much Monsanto irony, there's really nothing ironic at all when Monsanto's World Food Prize Laureate, Executive Vice President and Chief Technology Officer puts on a straight face and announces to the world that Monsanto's GM wheat "poses no concern."[1]

"Opinion surveys consistently report that consumers support FDA's current labeling policy – mandatory labeling for important nutrition or safety information. Food companies can and do provide additional information voluntarily to meet the preferences of their customers. Hundreds of organic or certified non-GM products are available for consumers who prefer these products. This approach offers choices for all consumers and does so without the risk of confusing consumers who are satisfied with the products they know, trust and can afford."
We're Monsanto

Lie #30: GMO Labels Would Only Confuse You[1]

Monsanto, the Biotechnology Industry Association, and a slew of other organizations don't want you to know what's in your food because—as they say—the labels would mislead and confuse you.[2]

Hmmm. Labeling foods with GMO labels—labels that nearly all Americans want—would confuse American consumers. Does that sort of logic confuse you?

More than sixty countries require GM labels.[3] Do GM labels confuse the three billion people in those countries?

Monsanto joined with several other anti-labeling corporations to spend some $45 million dollars in California to confuse voters with lies.[4]

Don't be confused. Monsanto and accomplices want to keep GMOs unlabeled because they know 93% of the people in the U.S.A. want GMO labeling.[5] The GMO peddlers know that when Europe labeled GMOs, food producers switched to non-GMO ingredients.[6] They don't want the same thing to happen in America.

Monsanto's lies are only confusing if you believe them.

Don't believe the lies! We have a right to know what's in our food.

"Want to hear something extraordinary?
Chances are, almost everything you've eaten
in your entire life was genetically modified."
We're Monsanto

Lie #31: Almost All Foods Are Genetically Modified[1]

Want to hear something extraordinary? Monsanto spinmeisters are full of manure. They want you to believe the lie that "the 'new' field of biotechnology ... isn't all that new." They want you to believe "it's been around for thousands of years."[2]

By Monsanto's definition, biotechnology and genetic modification are no different than traditional plant breeding. That's the song Monsanto sings with the FDA or when trying to persuade the public to buy and eat its mutant food. It sings a different song at the Patent and Trademark Office where its creations become so unique they deserve patent protections.[3]

Regardless of what song Monsanto sings, no farmer in the history of the world has ever inserted genes from bacteria into his or her crops. And until very recently, doing so wasn't possible. And until DNA became patentable, no one had any reason to do so.

The biotech industry loves to belittle anyone who's not bright enough to know that GMOs, and the processes by which GMOs are created, are substantially equivalent to natural plants created by natural means. Regardless, natural plants are not dependent on Roundup or chemical fertilizers.

For biotech scientists, "the birds and the bees" has nothing to do with sex; it's about using high-tech methods to combine genes from unrelated species in ways that never could occur in nature.

Perhaps there's irony in the fact that real birds and real bees thrive in a natural world with natural plants and natural plant breeding. And those same birds, bees, butterflies, etc., are dropping dead due to the environmental disaster that's encircling the globe due to genetically modified organisms and their accompanying poisons.[4-6]

According to Earth Open Source, "Genetic engineering is completely different from natural breeding and entails different risks. The genetic engineering and associated tissue culture processes are imprecise and highly mutagenic, leading to unpredictable changes in the DNA, proteins, and biochemical composition of the resulting GM crop that can lead to unexpected toxic or allergenic effects and nutritional disturbances."[7]

The FDA's own scientists clearly saw the differences between traditional and biotech products, and they "repeatedly warned that GM foods can create unpredictable, hard-to-detect side effects, including allergies, toxins, new diseases, and nutritional problems. They urged long-term safety studies, but were ignored."[8]

Andrew Kimbrell, the Executive Director of Center for Food Safety, is a public interest attorney, activist and author and has been named "one of the world's leading 100 visionaries."[9] What does Kimbrell have to say to the biotech industry about its claim that genetic engineering is the same as traditional breeding?

"Genetic engineering is to traditional crossbreeding what the nuclear bomb was to the sword."[10]

Lie #32: The FDA Said Prop 37 Would Mislead People[1]

What's inherently misleading is a No on 37 mailer that quotes the FDA making a statement that it didn't make.

FDA spokeswoman Morgan Liscinsky wrote, "The FDA has not made such statements with respect to Prop 37. We cannot speculate on Prop 37 and have no comments at this time."[2]

In addition to misquoting the FDA, the Yes on 37 campaign states, "the mailer's use of the FDA's official seal is a criminal offense. U.S. law says you can't misuse the seal of a government agency."[3]

Yes on 37 "also asked the U.S. Department of Justice to investigate the allegedly fraudulent misuse of FDA's seal in that mailer."[3]

"Major funding" for this "inherently misleading" mailer was provided by a large group of companies that want to mislead you regarding GMO labeling. Can you guess which company is the major funder?

"Proposition 37 is a ballot initiative . . . that would require a warning label on food products that include a genetically modified (GM) ingredient."
We're Monsanto

Lie #33: Labeling Initiatives Require Scary Warnings on GM Foods[1, 2]

Labeling initiatives would require warning labels on GM foods? Lie! Read some straight truth from Michele Simon, the author of *Appetite for Profit*: "No warning label would be required. Rather, the words 'partially produced with genetic engineering' or 'may be partially produced with genetic engineering' would be required on the back of the package—similar to what is now required for ingredient or allergen labeling. For whole foods, like the sweet corn coming soon to a Walmart near you, a sign would be posted on the store shelf with the words 'genetically engineered.' The aim is simply to offer consumers additional information about the contents of the foods they purchase."[3]

More truth. Monsanto knows that GMO labels on food are not warning labels, but they just as well could be. Norman Braksick, president of a Monsanto subsidary, knew it in 1994 when he said, "If you put a label on genetically engineered food you might as well put a skull and crossbones on it."[4] Now that we've got twenty years of research documenting the health risks associated with genetically modified foods, Braksick's death's head idea sounds like a good one.

Question: Since GMOs wreak havoc on our health—not to mention what they do to the health of the environment—and may contribute to premature death, why are GMOs in our food supply at all?

Answer: Monsanto.

▶ *Prop 37 would give consumers incomplete and misleading information*

Consumers rely on labels to provide factual, reliable and useful information, but the complex food labeling proposal in Prop 37 fails to meet those standards. An ill-conceived law, Prop 37 would impose confusing red tape requirements for labeling food products sold in California that do not exist in any other state or country in the world.

We're Monsanto

—Henry I. Miller, M.D., Stanford University

Founding Director, Office of Biotechnology of

US Food & Drug Administration

Lie #34: Stanford University Employs Henry Miller[1]

Let's talk about incomplete and misleading information. The No on 37 campaign used Henry Miller's credentials as a Stanford University professor to persuade California voters that "Prop 37 would give consumers incomplete and misleading information." They did so both with a TV ad and a campaign mailer. What's misleading about that? Miller isn't a Stanford University professor. Stanford was not pleased with the No on 37's "misleading information" and requested that the video be edited.[1]

Yes on 37 spokeswoman Stacy Malkan said that Stanford's request to edit the Miller video "is proof positive of the lack of credibility and lack of integrity of the No on 37 campaign."[1]

Monsanto was a major No on 37 funder.

It's possible that Monsanto and gangs' mistake was just an innocent oversight. But is it likely? If it were the first lie Monsanto had told, we might give it the benefit of the doubt.

But as for Monsanto and GMOs? No benefit! No Doubt!

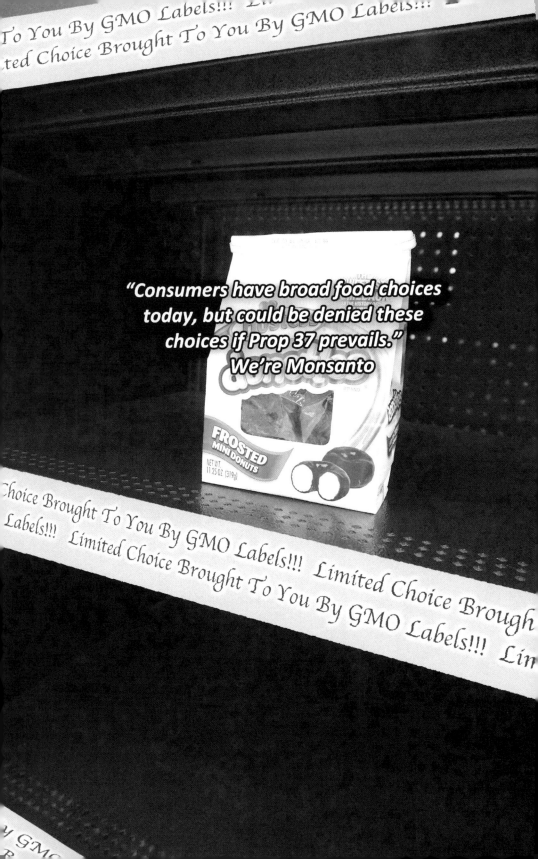

Lie #35: GMO Labels Will Limit Choice[1]

Monsanto wants you to believe that labeling GMOs would somehow limit your "broad food choices" in the supermarket.[1]

Don't think about this lie too long or your brain might explode. As Michele Simon states, "There is no basis in logic that consumers could be denied food choices. Indeed, Proposition 37 actually broadens the meaningful food choices available through greater transparency. Right now, people are eating in the dark."[2]

The Grocery Manufacturers Association, of which Monsanto is a member, is spreading the same lie in an attempt to defeat the State of Washington's labeling initiative.[3]

The editors of the pro-GMO website, Scientific American, shed some genetically modified light on the subject of GMO labels and consumer choice. When the European Union required labels in the late 1990s, major food producers switched to non-GM ingredients, which, they say, limited consumers' choice to buy GM ingredients—the same ingredients, by the way, that consumers had rejected. The editors lament the blessed fact that "Today it is virtually impossible to find GMOs in European supermarkets."[4]

Let's be perfectly clear: Labeling GMOs won't limit your choice, but it will limit Monsanto's power to keep three hundred million Americans in the dark. It's time to shine the light on Monsanto and related thugs. It's time to label GMOs.

No GMOs

"Proposition backers are opposed to modern medicine and sound science." – No on 37 We're Monsanto

Lie #36: People in Favor Of GMO Labels Oppose Medicine and Science[1]

California's Proposition 37 would have mandated GMO labeling ... had it not been beaten by the corporations that spread lies such as, "Proposition backers are opposed to modern medicine and sound science." These corporations want you to believe that "Health & Medical Experts Oppose the Flawed Food Labeling Proposition."[1]

Check out the list of health organizations that favor mandated GMO labeling: American Academy of Environmental Medicine, American College for Advancement in Medicine, American Holistic Medical Association, American Medical Students Association, American Public Health Association, Autism Spectrum Intervention Services and Training, Bernhoft Center for Advanced Medicine, Butte County Health Care Coalition, California Nurses Association, Canyon Springs Dental Group and Orthodontics, Chicago Eye Institute, Clinton Miller Health Freedom Advocates, Dominican Hospital (Formerly Catholic Healthcare West), Ebrahimian Integrative Dentistry, Foundations Therapy Service, Inc., Gerson Institute, Harbor Medical Group, Health-Ward Group LLC, Health Care without Harm, International College of Integrative Medicine, Latino Care Medical Group, Latino Diabetes Association, Layton Health Clinic, Linda Mar Vet. Hospital, Lyme Induced Autism Foundation, National Alliance for Mentally Ill-CA (NAMI-CA), National Health Federation, National Health Freedom Action, National Health Freedom Coalition, Pacific Center For

Integral Health, Palmetto Allergy and Asthma, Physicians Committee for Responsible Medicine, Physicians for Social Responsibility- Los Angeles, Physicians for Social Responsibility- Sacramento, Physicians for Social Responsibility- San Francisco Bay Area, Plaza Lane Optometry, Porter Ranch Medical Center, Practice Fusion, Preventive Medicine Research Institute, Redwood Wellness, San Francisco Preventive Medical Group, Santa Clara Medical Society, Santa Cruz Integrative Medicine, Santa Cruz Occupational Medical Center, Sunrise Dental.[2]

Are we expected to believe these medical organizations oppose "modern medicine and sound science?"

Or do you think maybe there's a chance their experience as medical professionals and their knowledge of "modern medicine and sound science" inform their opposition to GMOs and the corporations who insist on hiding them in our foods?

We read on the bottom of the No on 37 fact sheet: "Major funding by Monsanto Company, E.I. DuPont de Nemours & Co., Grocery Manufacturers Association (GMA) and more than 40 food company members. For a full list of donors visit www.NoProp37.com/donors."[1]

When you follow that link, you'll discover a list of 68 corporations that don't want you to know what's in your food. Can you guess how many of them are medical organizations?

That's right! You know the answer without even looking!

THANKS MONSANTO

"Interestingly, the main proponents of [GMO labeling] are special interest groups and individuals opposed to food biotechnology who are not necessarily engaged in the production of our nation's food supply."
We're Monsanto

Lie #37: The Main Proponents of GMO Labels Are Special Interest Groups[1]

Monsanto finds it interesting that "the main proponents of [GMO labeling] are special interest groups and individuals opposed to food biotechnology who are not necessarily engaged in the production of our nation's food supply."[1]

Interestingly, Monsanto's statement is a lie.

Many food producers, farmers and others who are very much "engaged in the production of our nation's food supply" support GMO labeling. Check out this list from California alone: Berkshire Co-op Market, Bozeman Community Food Co-op, BriarPatch Co-op Community Market, Burbank Certified Farmers' Market, Chico Natural Foods Cooperative, Co-Opportunity, Coastside Farmers' Markets, Davis Food Co-op, Dexter Lake Farmer's Market, Durango Natural Foods Co-op, Ecology Center Farmers' Markets, Encinitas Station Farmers Market, Ferry Plaza Farmers Market, Frontier Natural Products Co-op, Hayfork Farmers Market, Honest Weight Food Co-op, Hungry Hollow Co-op, Isla Vista Food Cooperative, La Montanita Co-op, Linden Hills Co-op, Mountain Lakes Organic Co-op, Mt. Shasta Farmer's Market, Natural Foods Co-op, New Leaf, New Leaf Market (Felton), Noe Valley Farmers Market, North Coast Co-op, North San Diego Certified Farmers Market, OC Green Market, Ocean Beach People's Organic Food Co-op, Other Avenues Cooperative Market, Otherworld Food Co-op, Inc., Pacifica Farmers' Market, People's Food Cooperative, Placerville Natural Food Co-op,

Rainbow Natural Grocery Cooperative, Rancho Santa Fe Farmers Market, Riverside Certified Farmer's Market, Sacramento Natural Foods Co-op, Scott Valley Certified Farmers' Market, Seward Co-op, Southern Humboldt Farmers Market, Spiral Foods Cooperative, Ukiah Natural Foods Co-op, Weaverville Farmers Market, Welk Farmers' Market, Westside Renaissance Market, Willy Street Co-op."[2]

Another interesting point about this particular lie is the kernel of truth it contains. Farmers produce food. Monsanto markets its genetically modified seeds and attendant poisons to farmers. You and I—food consumers—are nothing more than "individuals opposed to food biotechnology who are not necessarily engaged in the production of our nation's food supply." Monsanto doesn't care what consumers want. Worse than that, Monsanto stands in direct opposition to consumer preference.

Of course, Monsanto has to oppose consumer preference because our voices are growing louder every day, and this is what we're saying:

"Monsanto, get off our planet!"

Monsanto Profits

No GMO Labels   GMO Labels

"Economic studies indicate that I-522 would ultimately increase food costs for an average family by hundreds of dollars per year."
— NO on 522
We're Monsanto

Lie #38: GMO Labels Increase Costs [1, 2]

In 2012, Monsanto and the Biotechnology Industry Organization paid Boston-based Northbridge Environmental Management Consultants $55,000 to produce a study that Monsanto and buddies used to scare voters away from GM labeling in California. Among other things, the study claimed that GMO labels would increase a family's annual food cost as much as $400.[3]

Surprise! Surprise! In 2013, Big Food backed the No on 522 campaign using the same industry-funded lie in an attempt to convince Washington voters they can't afford to know what's in their food.[1]

How did Northbridge come up with the $400 figure? John Robbins, a lifelong food, animal, and environmental activist and best-selling author states, "This particular public relations company has no economists on its staff, has never done any work on economic analysis whatsoever. ... This company created some focus groups, and they tested different numbers to find out which number would be high enough to scare people, but not so high as to seem incredible, and lose validity in people's eyes. And that's how the number $400 was arrived at. The presumption was that it was arrived at by economic analysis. It was not."[4]

Zack Kaldveer and Ronnie Cummins also expose Monsanto's expensive lie about expensive food labeling for the lie that it is. They state that the same affidavit-based labeling system that is in place for "rBGH-free, trans fat-free, country of origin and fair trade" is the system that would be used to label GMO foods without economic impact on consumers.[5]

"We have used the affidavit system repeatedly, without undue burden or cost," said Trudy Bialic, Director of Public Affairs for Seattle-based PCC Natural Markets.[5]

"Megan Westgate, Executive Director of the Non-GMO Project confirmed what retailers who use the affidavit system said: 'An affidavit system like what's proposed in I-522 is a powerful way to have a significant impact on the food supply with minimal cost.'"[5]

Monsanto pumped in $8 million dollars to convince California voters they couldn't afford to know what's in their food.[6] It's willing to spend that sort of money, not because it cares about your struggles with your food bills, but because it knows it's going to struggle to pay its own bills when GMOs are finally labeled.

In other words, Monsanto only cares about your food bills when your food choices cut into its profit margin.

It's time to cut Monsanto's profit margin down to zero by labeling its altered and poisoned products.

But that's only the first step. Next we need to eliminate open-field testing and marketing of GM plants, animals, and foods.

It's time to stand up to the world's biggest bully and cut Monsanto from our lives.

"Monsanto should not have to vouchsafe the safety of biotech food. Our interest is in selling as much of it as possible. Assuring its safety is the FDA's job."
We're Monsanto

Lie #39: Biotech Food Safety Is Not Monsanto's Responsibility[1]

You might think Phil Angell, Monsanto's director of corporate communications, would have been fired when he told best selling author, Michael Pollan "Monsanto should not have to vouchsafe the safety of biotech food."[1] His statement directly contradicts the following Monsanto PR propaganda: "Before we submit a biotech crop to regulatory agencies for approval, it has undergone numerous tests by our research teams to ensure and prove it's as safe as its conventional equivalent."[2]

But, no, he wasn't fired. After all, Monsanto knows that different situations call for different lies.

Case in point. When Monsanto presents a new transgenic product for FDA review, it tells the FDA that Monsanto research has proven the product is safe. (Remember that Monsanto people/players infest and infect the FDA like Roundup resistant super weeds infest the American landscape.) Then the FDA turns around and tells Monsanto that the product in question is safe because Monsanto says it's safe. Twisted? Yes. Read the following excerpt from an FDA letter addressed to Monsanto: "Based on the safety and nutritional assessment you have conducted, it is our understanding that Monsanto has concluded that corn products derived from this new variety are not materially different in composition, safety, and other relevant parameters from corn currently on the market, and that the genetically modified corn does not raise issues that would require premarket review or approval by FDA. ... As you are aware, it is Monsanto's responsibility to ensure that foods marketed by the firm are safe, wholesome and in compliance with all applicable legal and regulatory requirements."[3]

So there you have it. Monsanto tells you and me that it is not responsible for the safety of its unnatural life forms. It tells you, me, and the FDA that its unnatural life forms are safe. The FDA tells Monsanto the altered life forms are safe because Monsanto says they're safe.

Does any of that mess make you feel safe? We are safe only in our knowledge that Monsanto continues to feed the world a steady diet of poisons and lies.

"We are sympathetic with people who believe they have been injured and understand their concern to find the cause, but reliable scientific evidence indicates that Agent Orange is not the cause of serious long-term health effects."
We're Monsanto

Lie #40: Agent Orange Does Not Cause Serious Health Effects[1]

Apparently 150,000 Vietnamese babies weren't included in the studies. Neither were the 800,000 Vietnamese people who "suffer serious health problems as a result" of Agent Orange.[1] Neither were the 2.5 million American soldiers exposed to Agent Orange, thousands of whom have applied for and received a few thousand bucks in exchange for their destroyed health.[2] Neither were Monsanto's own employees back in the 1940s who suffered and died from the effects of exposure to dioxin.[3]

Yes, the 1940s! Monsanto knew back then, and it took a rigged Monsanto study and some propaganda to convince the world otherwise. That rigged study later formed the scientific basic for denying Vietnam veterans compensation for their "serious long-term health effects."[4]

The 1940s! That means Monsanto knew when it "dumped 30 to 40 pounds of dioxin a day into the Mississippi River between 1970 and 1977 which could enter the St. Louis food chain." It knew when it allowed many dioxin contaminated consumer products including Lysol to be sold in the USA for over thirty years.[3]

Of course Monsanto knew. It "told the EPA that it wasn't able to use it's own labs to test products for dioxin because it was too toxic to handle."[3]

"Too toxic to handle" or "not the cause of serious long-term health effects?"

Maybe Monsanto can claim that dioxin does not cause "serious long-term health effects" because it does not consider the following conditions to be either "serious" or "long-term": prostate cancer, respiratory cancers, multiple myeloma, type II diabetes, Hodgkin's disease, non-Hodgkin's lymphoma, soft tissue sarcoma, chloracne, porphyria cutanea tarda, peripheral neuropathy, chronic lymphocytic leukemia, and spina bifida, liver cancer; lipid metabolism disorder; reproductive abnormalities and congenital deformities such as cleft lip, cleft palate, club foot, hydrocephalus, neural tube defects, fused digits, muscle malformations and paralysis; and some developmental disabilities.[5]

Get serious, Monsanto!

Any guess on when Monsanto finally admitted Agent Orange *does* sicken and kill people?

1975? No.

2004? No

Now? No. Even in 2013, Monsanto's official position is that "a causal connection linking Agent Orange to chronic disease in humans has not been established ... ."[6]

Wow! Same lie since the 1940s!

If Monsanto will lie for three quarters of a century about one of the most deadly compounds on Earth, how long do you think it will lie about GMOs?

It really doesn't matter because we have over 100 years of scientific evidence that Monsanto's poison peddlers are serious, long-term liars. That's all we really need to know.

"There is no need for, or value in testing the safety of GM foods in humans."

"The fact is, biotech crops have been reviewed and tested more than any crop in the history of agriculture and, each time, the result has been the same: they are safe."

We're Monsanto

Lie #41: No Need to Test for Safety of GM Foods in Humans[1]

Monsanto makes the following claims: 1. "There is no need for, or value in testing the safety of GM foods in humans."[1]

2. "The fact is, biotech crops have been reviewed and tested more than any crop in the history of agriculture and, each time, the result has been the same: they are safe."[2]

The beauty in these lies is that they contradict each other. Monsanto says out of one side of its mouth there is no need for or value in testing the safety of GM foods in humans. Then, out of the other side, that biotech crops have been reviewed and tested more than any crop in the history of agriculture and, each time, the result has been the same: they are safe. Not tested vs. tested more than any crop in the history of agriculture and always found to be safe. Which is it? Neither. Both are lies. Of course there is a need and value in testing the safety of GM foods in humans. And whatever limited testing Monsanto performs—none on humans, by the way, except for the worldwide experiment Monsanto continues to conduct on all of us without our consent—Monsanto constructs its studies to cover-up problems.[3]

Dr. Arpad Pusztai speaks with authority regarding Monsanto's sham animal feeding studies. The UK government had commissioned Pusztai—the top expert in the field of lectin proteins—to lead a team of researchers with the prestigious Rowett Institute conducting long-term animal feeding studies prior to introducing GMOs into Europe. The researchers initially believed their GM potato would not harm the experimental rats. They were surprised when their furry subjects "developed potentially precancerous cell growth in the digestive tract, inhibited development of their brains, livers, and testicles, partial atrophy of the liver, enlarged pancreases and intestines, and immune system damage."[4] Pusztai was beyond surprised after he reviewed the experiments that provided the basis for the approval of GM foods in Europe. "This was the first time I realized what flimsy evidence was being presented to the committee. There was missing data, poor research design, and very superficial tests indeed. Theirs was a very unconvincing case. And some of the work was really very poorly done. I want to impress on you, it was a real shock."[5] Pusztai was shocked because he had believed the lie that Monsanto scientists uphold scientific standards of objectivity and independence. Pusztai was further shocked when he was fired and given a gag order after announcing on European TV that, based on his own animal feeding research, he would not eat transgenic foods.[5]

It was the public's turn to be shocked in 2012 when Professor Gilles-Eric Seralini and his team of scientists released photos of rats bulging with cancerous tumors—tumors that resulted after being fed genetically modified corn and the same level of Roundup authorized in drinking water.[6] (See preceding full-page photo.) Rather than repeat Pusztai's and Seralini's experiments, the pro-biotech industry responded with lies, distortions, and spin.[7, 8]

Seralini is fighting back. In September 2013, he hit the speaking circuit addressing the public in London, Edinburgh, Manchester, Newport and Cardiff. He also held discussions with UK, Welsh and Scottish parliamentarians. He accused the UK Food Standards Agency (FSA) of "recklessly endangering public health" by not demanding long-term testing of GMO foods. "Our research found severe toxicity from GM maize and [Monsanto pesticide] Roundup. The British Food Standards Agency has uncritically accepted the European Food Safety Authority's dismissal of the study, even though many of EFSA's experts have been exposed as having conflicts of interest with the GM industry. At the very least, the British government should demand long-term mandatory safety testing on all GM foods before they are released onto the market."[9]

Shicana Allen authored an article titled, "This little piggy was fed GMOs," published in *The Bulletin*, a Toronto journal. Allen writes, "Dr. Judy Carman, associate professor in Health and the Environment at Flinders University (Adelaide, South Australia) and a team of seven other co-authors and scientists have released results of a long-term, peer-reviewed toxicology study that has found even more adverse effects resulting from the consumption of genetically modified foods.

....

"Dr. Carman and her team discovered a 25% increase in uterus weight in the animals fed the GM diet as compared to the control group. In addition, GM-fed male pigs were four times more likely to be afflicted with severe stomach inflammation, while females had more than double the risk of the control group. The doctor emphasized that both the uterus and stomach findings were biologically and statistically significant. There was also a 'marginally significant change on a measure of liver health in the blood of GM-fed pigs.'"[10]

In addition, numerous farmers report severe health effects in their GMO-fed animals.[11] Danish pig farmer, Ib Borup Pedersen, is one. Pedersen "routinely observed the detrimental effects of GM soy feed on his herd. He also noticed a relationship between Roundup herbicide residues and stillbirths and malformations in his pig litters.

"Pedersen's findings, released in April 2012, caused much discussion in Europe's largest pig industry and led to the Danish government commissioning new research on the safety of GM feed."[12]

What's the moral of the story? It's no shock when Monsanto lies about the safety of GMOs and Roundup. And it's no shock when Monsanto lies about the scientists and others who have the courage to tell the public about Monsanto and its lies.

Lie #42: Monsanto Is a New Company[1]

Monsanto President Hendrik A. Verfaillie addressed the Farm Journal Conference in 2000 just after Monsanto had merged with Pharmacia. Without actually mentioning Monsanto's various crimes against humanity, Verfaillie announced that Monsanto had the opportunity to change its "behavior" and "actions" because "Monsanto is a new company," and it should be measured from that time forward on how well they made that change.

Several years have passed since Verfaillie announced the birth of a new and improved Monsanto. Let's do as he advised and measure the change.

First off, if Monsanto were serious about recreating itself, it would have done so, not by closing the door on yesteryears' victims (that's what Monsanto has always done), but by fully compensating those victims, which, of course, would be impossible. How does one compensate every human being on the planet for the PCBs we carry within our bodies?[2] How could it ever pay the costs associated with Agent Orange, dioxin, DDT, etc.?

How did Monsanto executives deal with its pollution, corruption, victims, and liability of the past? They buried it, along with its debt-burdened subsidiary, Solutia. *Bloomberg* reports, "Monsanto created Solutia as a vehicle to dump massive environmental liabilities generated decades before the spinoff."[3]

Then it had two brief affairs with other companies, before launching itself in agriculture, bringing with it its expertise at destroying and killing.[4]

Old Monsanto was known for its global pollution, corruption, legal issues, and endless lies. New Monsanto is known for its global pollution, corruption, aggressive legal action against farmers, endless lies, and blatant disregard and contempt for the desires of millions of people around the world who neither need nor want Monsanto's poison-saturated genetically modified products.

As seen in the following 2013 statement by Monsanto, its attempt to separate itself from its shameful past surpasses the bizarre: "In 2002, Monsanto Company was incorporated as an independent, public company focused solely on seeds and agricultural products. The manufacture of Agent Orange by a former company of the same name occurred over 40 years ago."[5]

We, the people of the world, are fed up with Monsanto feeding us poison, corruption, and bizarre lies. How fed up? *The Nation* reported in 2012, "Geneva-based Covalence ranked the company dead last of 581 multinationals in its 2010 reputation and ethics index, which is distributed by Reuters and Bloomberg."[4]

Most makeovers are only skin-deep. As hard as Monsanto tried, it couldn't shed its old skin because it had nothing with which to replace it. Monsanto is Monsanto. If there is any difference between then and now, it is this: Monsanto will only survive if we actually eat its poisons and lies. And humanity will only survive if we don't.

"This technology increases your crop yields, in some cases dramatically so."
We're Monsanto

Lie #43: Biotechnology Increases Crop Yields[1]

Monsanto's former President and CEO, Hendrik A. Verfaillie, told farmers in 2000 that biotechnology "increases your crop yields, in some cases dramatically so."[1]

In 2013, Monsanto Chief Technology Officer, Dr. Robb Fraley wrote, "When I was on our family farm in Illinois in the 1970s, a 100-bushel corn crop would put a smile on my dad's face. In that same part of the country today, in 2009, it takes a 180- or 200-bushel corn crop to produce that smile. In that short amount of time, we've effectively seen yields double."[2]

Impressive! Impressive that Verfaillie and Fraley credit biotechnology with increased yields. Nearly all genetically engineered crops are engineered to either absorb or produce poison.[3] Neither toxic trait increases yield. The increases Fraley speaks of are due to traditional breeding practices, not genetic engineering.

Furthermore, University of Canterbury researchers "analyzed data on agricultural productivity in North America and Western Europe over the last 50 years" and found biotechnology is a failing technology on every front. Conventional staple crop production consistently out produces biotechnology. And it does so with less pesticide and fertilizer.[4]

The Canterbury team leader, Professor Jack Heinemann, states, "We found that US yield in non-GM wheat is also falling further behind Europe, demonstrating that American choices in biotechnology penalise both GM and non-GM crop types relative to Europe.

"Agriculture responds to commercial and legislative incentive systems. These take the form of subsidies, intellectual property rights instruments, tax incentives, trade promotions and regulation. The incentive systems in North America are leading to a reliance on GM seeds and management practices that are inferior to those being adopted under the incentive systems in Europe.

"The decrease in annual variation in yield suggests that Europe has a superior combination of seed and crop management technology and is better suited to withstand weather variations. This is important because annual variations cause price speculations that can drive hundreds of millions of people into food poverty.

"We need more than agriculture; we need agricultures—a diversity of practices for growing and making food that GM does not support; we need systems that are useful, not just profit-making biotechnologies—we need systems that provide a resilient supply to feed the world well."[4]

In addition to GMOs' decreased yield, we need to remember that GMOs also result in decreased quality. Roundup resistant crops resist Roundup, but they are far from immune to the effects of Roundup.

De Dell Seed Company (Canada's only non-GMO seed company) conducted research that found stunning differences between GM corn and conventional corn. Among other differences, sampled non-GMO corn had 437 times more calcium, 56 times more magnesium, and 7 times more manganese than GMO corn.[5]

What would account for GM corn's nutritional epic fail? Roundup kills weeds by blocking the absorption of soil nutrition. In other words, Roundup starves plants to death.[6] Roundup resistant plants manage to stay alive, but they also absorb fewer nutrients resulting in nutritionally deficient seeds and food products.[5]

Then of course, we can't forget that these nutritionally deficient and sometimes visibly different foods are also saturated with Roundup, Monsanto's premier poison that wreaks havoc on human and animal health.[7]

Through the wonders of GMOs, farmers get to enjoy the benefits of decreased yield, while consumers enjoy decreased nutrition and increased ingestion of poisons. How could Monsanto ever manage to profit from such a package?

With lie after lie.

"I do not have favors I need to repay to people who have been in Washington for years." – Mitt Romney
We're Monsanto

Lie #44: Romney Has No Favors to Repay[1]

Superman sports the letter S on his chest. Hester Prynne wore a Scarlet A on hers to warn her neighbors of her sin. And the media painted the letter M on Mitt Romney's chest to warn Americans of his Mormon religion. But Romney and a host of other high-level political figures should wear another M on their chests for another reason, an M that stands for Monsanto. And if a greater connection to the chemical giant warrants a bigger letter, Romney's M may rank among the largest in Washington DC.

Monsanto was one of Bain & Company's and Romney's first clients. Aviva Shen reports, "From 1977 to 1985, Romney helped navigate Monsanto through very rocky waters. The agribusiness was flooded with lawsuits after Congress banned the toxic coolant PCBs, a Monsanto product that has been linked to cancer and neurological disorders. At the same time, Monsanto's Agent Orange toxin, used to defoliate jungles in the Vietnam War, was linked to the contamination of millions of Vietnamese and American soldiers and had been dubbed 'the largest chemical warfare operation' in human history. ... Monsanto relied on Romney to create their new public image — one that did not involve poisoning soldiers or dumping chemicals in rivers."[2]

The Nation ran a lengthy article titled "Mitt Romney, Monsanto Man" highlighting Romney's connections to Monsanto. According to the article author, Wayne Barrett, "John W. Hanley, the Monsanto CEO at the time, has said how 'impressed' he was with the 30-year-old Mitt. Hanley became so close to Romney that he and Romney's boss Bill Bain devised the idea of creating Bain Capital as a way of keeping Romney in the fold. Unless Mitt was allowed to run this spin-off venture firm, Hanley and Bain feared, he would leave. Hanley even contributed $1 million to Romney's first investment pool at Bain Capital. Monsanto's Hanley is in fact the only business executive outside of the Bain founding family to so shape Romney's career—jumpstarting the two companies, Bain & Company and Bain Capital, that account for all but two years of Romney's much-ballyhooed business experience."[3]

Wow! In the comics, Superman fought against the CEO/scientist/philanthropist/sociopath, Lex Luthor. In real life, Romney helped Monsanto shed its responsibility for its toxic past and helped recreate a new Monsanto by hiding its sociopathic business practices behind a fabricated image of philanthropic scientists. But that was years ago. At the time of the presidential election, did Romney still align himself with Monsanto? The word "align" doesn't quite do justice to this situation. Romney's connections to Monsanto and friends run so deep and so wide, we might more accurately state that Romney had immersed himself in an army of Monsanto loyalists.[3] What about Romney's claim that he doesn't have favors he needs to repay? "According to OpenSecrets.org, Mitt Romney has taken $4,075,531 in campaign contributions from America agribusinesses."[4] Hmmm. That's a whole lot of favor-less money. The world will never know what might have happened if Romney had won the election. But if Romney's thirty-five year old love affair with Monsanto and its money had played a part in his presidential politics, we might safely assume that Romney's devotion to Monsanto would have played a much bigger role than his devotion to his religion.

Reducing Regulatory Barriers

"So you guys are leading the way, and we know there are some things government can do to help clear the way for your success. We can make sure America remains the best place on Earth to do business by knocking down barriers that stand in the way of your growth. That's why we passed 17 different tax cuts for small businesses, why I proposed lowering the corporate tax rate and eliminating unnecessary regulations to help larger businesses create jobs."

—President Obama, February 2011

Strategic Objective: Develop and reform regulations to reduce barriers, increase the speed and predictability of regulatory processes, and reduce costs while protecting human and environmental health.

Regulations governing our health products and services, energy production, national security, food, and en some
long ology
and ations
may not have kept pace. Clear, predic security, and
efficacy of products of biological research are powerful drivers of R&D investments by all sectors. In addition, because externalities and social attitudes influence market opportunities in the bioeconomy as they do in other economic arenas, a clear understanding of the benefits and risks of bioproducts is critical to the future bioeconomy.

"Here's what I'll do as president . . . we'll let folks know whether their food has been genetically modified because Americans should know what they're buying." —Barack Obama, 2007 We're Monsanto

Lie #45: Obama Will Label GMOs[1]

Prior to getting elected, Barack Obama promised the American people in 2007 he'd get genetically modified foods labeled "because Americans should know what they're buying."[1] Here is what Obama has done since:

• Appointed Michael Taylor as the FDA Food Czar. Jeffrey Smith writes that Taylor "may be responsible for more food-related illness and death than anyone in history."[2] Smith also writes, "Taylor was formerly the outside attorney for the biotech giant Monsanto, and later became their vice president. He had also been the counsel for the International Food Biotechnology Council (IFBC), for whom he drafted a model of government policy designed to rush GMOs onto the market with no significant regulations. The final FDA policy that he oversaw, which did not require any safety tests or labeling, closely resembled the model he had drafted for the IFBC."[3]

• Appointed at least six other biotech-friendly people to key positions. Two of these people include Roger Beachy, who moved directly from his position with the Monsanto Danforth Center to his position as director of the National Institute of Food and Agriculture, and Tom Vilsack as U.S. Secretary of Agriculture whose credentials include "founder and former chair of the Governor's Biotechnology Partnership," and recipient of the *Governor of the Year* award from The Biotechnology Industry Organization.[4]

• Permitted the approval of at least 10 genetically modified crops including "Monsanto's GMO alfalfa, sugar beets, and Bt soy; Syngenta's GMO corn for ethanol, and Bt cotton; and Pioneer's GMO soybeans."[4] Regarding

Monsanto's GM alfalfa and sugar beets, The co-founder of Morninglory Farm, Robbie Hanna Anderman, writes in a Tikkun article, "President Barack Obama pushed the Secretary of Agriculture and the U.S. Department of Agriculture to deregulate genetically engineered alfalfa and sugar beets in the United States. The USDA came through as he directed, totally deregulating these Monsanto-patented genes."[5]

• Authorized the 2012 "National Bioeconomy Blueprint" in which the White House lays out its full support of genetic engineering and the corporations that produce them.[6]

• "Knowingly signed the Monsanto Protection Act in 2013 over the insistence of more than 250,000 Americans who signed an urgent letter asking that he use his executive authority to veto H.R. 933 and send it back to Congress to remove the Monsanto Protection Act from the bill."[1]

There's something warped about the way President Obama used his GMO-labeling promise to strengthen the stranglehold Monsanto has throughout the chambers of governments worldwide.

Anderman makes a statement that resonates with many of Obama's grassroots and organic former supporters: "When Obama cried, 'Yes, we can!' he obviously was speaking for a different 'we' than those who voted for him imagined."[5]

"Monsanto is committed to participating constructively in the political process, as such participation is essential to the Company's long-term success."
We're Monsanto

Lie #46: Monsanto Participates Constructively in Politics[1]

We Americans get passionate over our presidential elections. Both parties demonize their opponents while deifying their own candidate. What we fail to realize is that, more often than not in recent years, both major candidates earned their places on their party's respective ticket by supporting the corporations that support their political careers.[2] And when the same corporation supports both candidates, we can argue and debate until the genetically modified corn-fed cows come home, but when the votes are counted and the president is sworn in, the corporation wins and democracy loses.

In 2012, Monsanto's man Obama ran against Monsanto's man Romney. Both have the same hypocritical food policies: serve organic foods at home while serving the biotech industry at work.[3] And while they're serving the biotech industry, the industry serves the American people the illusion of choice. As the author and political lecturer G. Ed Griffin states, "Yes, you've got a left wing and a right wing, but they're just opposite wings of the same ugly bird."[4] As far as America's food and current food policies are concerned, Monsanto constructed a turnkey presidential race in 2012, a race it couldn't lose. And now it continues its 30+ year reign as one of the real rulers of the United States of America. Some even call it the United States of Monsanto.[5]

"Giving is a natural part of what we do at Monsanto. As a company, we are committed to making lives better."
We're Monsanto

Lie #47: Giving Is Natural For Monsanto[1]

There's no question that Monsanto gives much through its philanthropic efforts, but what, to whom, and why does it give? How much has the Monsanto Fund given to Monsanto victims? None.

None to the countless Vietnamese who continue to suffer from the horrifying effects of Agent Orange. None to PCB saturated Anniston, Alabama. None to the organic farmers whose farms have been destroyed from GM contamination. None for the cleanup of 56 contaminated Superfund sites. None to the widows or families of dead Indian cotton farmers.[2] (See preceding image.) And none to the family of "Silvino Talavera, an 11-year-old from Paraguay who died days after breathing in a cloud of Monsanto's Roundup herbicide sprayed by a crop duster."[3] Giving to its victims would be the right thing to do, but for Monsanto, giving the impression of doing good is really more important than doing it. Monsanto fakes goodness through predatory philanthropy. We see it in action when Monsanto offers "free" seeds to countries in crisis. Of course, once farmers are locked into Monsanto's licensing agreement, they are forced to purchase expensive Monsanto seeds and poisons year after year, which "places unbearable economic burden on the poor farmers."[2]

Silvia Ribeiro, Latin America Director for ETC, an Action Group on Erosion, Technology and Concentration, states, "The notion that farmers in the South will benefit from post-patent GE seeds is patently absurd. Under the guise of charity, the Gene Giants are devising new schemes to soften opposition to transgenics and reach new markets. In reality, the Gene Giants don't have the capacity or the interest to supply the diversity needed in sustainable farming systems or to meet the urgent need for locally adapted varieties, especially in the face of climate change."[4]

Absurd or not, Monsanto seized an opportunity following the 2010 earthquake in Haiti to capture new markets "under the guise of charity."[4] Haiti saw through Monsanto's ruse. "Chavannes Jean-Baptiste, the Executive Director of MPP and the spokesperson for the National Peasant Movement of the Congress of Papay (MPNKP), called the entry of Monsanto seeds into Haiti 'a very strong attack on small agriculture, on farmers, on biodiversity, on Creole seeds ... and on what is left our environment in Haiti.'" Haiti's "Ministry of Agriculture rejected Monsanto's offer of Roundup Ready GM seeds."[5]

Haiti's 'No' to Monsanto brings to mind Mahatma Gandhi's statement: "A 'No' uttered from the deepest conviction is better than a 'Yes' merely uttered to please, or worse, to avoid trouble."[6] Gandhi made another well-known statement: "We must be the change we wish to make in this world."[7]

Monsanto proclaims, "As the philanthropic arm of Monsanto, we're focused on one goal – strengthening both farming communities and the communities where we live and work."[7] Considering the fact that Monsanto's corporate practices systematically destroy farms and farmers around the world and have resulted in hopeless debt and contributed to the deaths of more than a quarter of a million Indian farmers, do you think Gandhi would have been pleased to know that Monsanto uses his "be the change" statement on its Monsanto Fund website?[7]

MONSANTO

"At Monsanto, we place value on doing things the right way—openly, honestly and with the utmost respect and integrity."
We're Monsanto

Lie #48: Monsanto Values Doing Things the Right Way[1]

Some Monsanto deceptions merit a thoughtful and lengthy response. Others are best addressed at a visceral level. But from time to time Monsanto tells an especially repugnant whopper. And on those special occasions, the best response moves on down the gut before emerging quite appropriately from the back end of a genetically modified corn-fed cow.

Consider the following whopper: "At Monsanto, we place value on doing things the right way—openly, honestly and with the utmost respect and integrity."[1]

Entire books have been dedicated to exposing Monsanto, its lies, and its numerous atrocities against humanity and the environment.[2-4] No doubt, numerous others will follow.

There are several reasons to study such books. One good reason is this: Once you know that Monsanto feeds the world lie after lie, you free yourself from the power of its lies. Then you're free to think, feel, vote, buy, and act independently from its bullshit.

"In 2008 Monsanto made a commitment to sustainable agriculture – pledging to produce more, conserve more, and improve farmers' lives by 2030."
We're Monsanto

Lie #49: Monsanto Is Committed to Sustainable Agriculture[1]

According to Monsanto, sustainable agriculture is the solution to the impending global famine, and Monsanto will provide that solution, or at least it commits to do so by 2030. Although 2030 was more than two decades into the future when Monsanto made that lofty commitment, it doesn't stop the company's spinmeisters from currently declaring Monsanto to be "A Sustainable Agriculture Company."[2]

2030 or now, sustainable agriculture is incompatible with Monsanto's mission to produce profits. Its entire business model is designed to force farmers and hence consumers to be dependent upon Monsanto's unsustainable agricultural system and products.

In Monsanto's "sustainable" world, Monsanto holds patents and collects royalties on all seeds from now into eternity, the ancient and sustainable practice of seed saving is a crime, and terminator technology mandates compliance. In Monsanto's world, it alters all seeds to tolerate its soil-killing poisons and fertilizers, making it necessary for farmers to purchase ever more poisons and fertilizers. In Monsanto's world, its over-priced seeds drive poor farmers to suicide, its monocrops destroy family farms and biodiversity, while taxpayers subsidize these destructive and unsustainable practices.

Dr. Joseph Mercola isn't impressed with Monsanto's unsustainable business model. "Far from being life sustaining," Mercola writes, "our modern chemical-dependent farming methods strip soil of nutrients, destroy critical soil microbes, contribute to desertification and global climate change, and saturate farmlands with toxic pesticides, herbicides and fertilizers that then migrate into ground water, rivers, lakes and oceans."[3]

Even the US Department of Agriculture (USDA) pointed out in 2012 that our current monoculture-dominated landscape is unsustainable in the long term.[3]

Obviously, Monsanto's system of agriculture is not sustainable. It was never intended to be sustainable. Predatory corporations like Monsanto extract, exploit, and profit from natural resources until those resources are gone. Then they take their money and run.

Unfortunately, they won't run far once they've killed the soil, polluted the water, and exhausted the world's supply of phosphorous. Monsanto's end game will likely result in the very thing Monsanto claims it is committed to averting: global famine.[4]

So what's the real solution to increased food needs?

81 Councillors of the World Future Council, who "form a voice for the rights of future generations," made this statement: "The United Nations, through its Office of the Special Rapporteur on the Right to Food, has documented ecological agriculture's potential in hungry regions to double food production in one decade. Chaired by former World Food Prize awardee Dr. Hans Herren, the 2008 International Assessment of Agricultural Knowledge, Science and Technology for Development (IAASTD) report, developed by 400 experts and endorsed by 59 governments, calls for redirection of agricultural development toward such sustainable practices.

Agroecology and food sovereignty are emerging solutions shaped and chosen by scientists and citizens worldwide."[5]

The human race stands at a crossroads. We either return to and further develop ecological farming practices, nurture our soil, and preserve our water, or we continue to give Monsanto free reign to patent and engineer plants, exploit resources, strap poor farmers with insurmountable debt, kill the soil and pollinators, pollute the water, and monopolize our food system.

One path sustains life while honoring the earth, nature, and biodiversity. The other path destroys life while honoring short-term corporate profits.[6]

We're talking about the earth, Monsanto! We're not going to let you destroy it!

Lie #50: You Can Trust Monsanto[1]

Best selling author, Michael Pollan, asked Jerry Hjelle, Monsanto's vice president for regulatory affairs, about problems associated with Bt crops. Pollan summed up their conversation this way: "Hjelle told me that resistance should not unduly concern us since 'there are a thousand other Bt's out there' — other insecticidal proteins. 'We can handle this problem with new products,' he said. 'The critics don't know what we have in the pipeline.'"

And then Hjelle followed up with the phrase, "Trust us."

No problem!

If there is one thing the people of the world have learned over the past one hundred years, it is this: We trust you, Monsanto, because you *are* Monsanto, feeding the world, lie after lie.

Conclusion

Monsanto lies.

Monsanto-paid scientists, lobbyists, government officials, media, and fellow food industry bullies continue to spread its lies. Every time we buy a Monsanto product, we give Monsanto more power to create more unnatural life forms, bribe government officials, buy out competitors, conduct unethical "scientific" research, manipulate "scientific" findings, discredit independent scientific research, fight against GMO labeling, sue farmers, harass independent media, fight law suits, collude with the U.S. government in forcing Iraqi farmers to use its seeds, provide "free" seeds of extortion to the world's poorest people, harass, threaten and control the media, collude with willing governments, strong-arm and threaten unwilling governments, pay off shareholders, pollute the world, and then lie about all of it.

With that in mind, there is no moral justification to buy any product grown with Monsanto poisons.

None! Ever!

Don't buy its unnatural life forms. Don't buy its other poisons. Don't buy its lies.

Monsanto infests the world's government chambers and farmers' fields because, even today, few people know or care about Monsanto.

You can change that.

Join with the millions of people around the world who have already committed to March Against Monsanto.

Spread the word in any way you are able. Tell your friends, family, and neighbors about Monsanto. Use social media, rally, protest, write government officials, give presentations, pass around this book.

In conclusion, keep in mind these words from Jeffrey Smith: an Alabama "court found Monsanto guilty of negligence, wantonness, suppression of the truth, nuisance, trespass, and outrage. Outrage, according to Alabama law, usually requires conduct 'so outrageous in character and extreme in degree as to go beyond all possible bounds of decency so as to be regarded as atrocious and utterly intolerable in civilized society.'"1

Monsanto was and is:

• Outrageous!
• Extreme in degree!
• Beyond all possible bounds of decency!
• Atrocious! and
• Utterly intolerable in civilized society!

Together, we can stop Monsanto.

Together, we must stop Monsanto before Monsanto stops the world.

March Against Monsanto Photo Credits

(Justin Zern took the photos on Kauai, Hawaii, on March 9 and July 31, 2013, and the photos on Molokai, Hawaii, on March 30, 2013. All other photos were taken on May 25, 2013, the date of the first global March Against Monsanto.)

• Introduction, Zakiyya Ismail, Johannesburg, South Africa
• Lies #1-9, Alex GD, Brussels, Belgium
• Lies #12-13, Annie Beechum, Denver, Colorado, USA
See more at:
https://www.facebook.com/media/set/?set=a.253093184830910.1073741841.231143710359191&type=3
• Lie #14, Bob Ramsak, Quito, Ecuador
See more at: http://pirancafe.com/2013/05/25/march-against-monsanto-in-quito-notebook-and-22-photos/
• Lie #17, Bobbi Jordan, Sitka, Alaska, USA
• Lie #18, Debi Terry, Sitka, Alaska, USA
• Lie #19, Christopher Aultman, Greenville, South Carolina, USA
See more at:
https://plus.google.com/u/0/112003581826344544912/posts/TsfanvzTQMN
• Lie #20, 23-28, Justin Zern, Kauai & Molokai, Hawaii, USA
See more Kauai photos at:
https://www.facebook.com/justin.zern/media_set?set=a.567095053314330.1073741829.100000415210705&type=3
See more Molokai photos at:
https://www.facebook.com/justin.zern/media_set?set=a.576823715674797.1073741833.100000415210705&type=3

• Lies #29-37, Matty Moo McAlpine, Brisbane, Queensland, Australia

See more at:

https://www.facebook.com/alpha00012/media_set?set=a. 10151609877088948.1073741825.737223947&type=1

• Lie #38, Paula Kirman, Edmonton, Alberta, Canada

• Lies #39, 40, 42, 43, Rich Fought, Seattle, Washington, USA

• Lie #44, Survival Doc, St. Louis, Missouri, USA

• Lie #45, 47, 49, 50, Zakiyya Ismail, Johannesburg, South Africa

See more at:

https://plus.google.com/u/0/photos/1073006994136807 27443/albums/5884834837840323585

Full Page "Lie" Photo Credits

• Lie #1: (Woman's Hands Holding Empty Bowl) Brett Wilcox

• Lie #2: (Dead Zone Image) NASA Photo

• Lie #3: (Monsanto Man Pointing Finger At Farmer) Mikelann & Brett Wilcox

• Lie #4: (Monarch Butterfly On Roundup Container) Monarch © Depositphotos.com/Dennis Sabo #5940611. Roundup, Brett Wilcox

• Lie #5: (Mannequin, World Food Domination Prize) Brett Wilcox

• Lie #6: (Kids Playing On Grass Near Roundup) Brett Wilcox

• Lie #7: ("Family and neighbors of Vijay Thamke grieve over his body at his home before it is taken away for the cremation. A farmer from Sonbardi village, he committed suicide on 27 March 2010." 7/32)
Prashant Panjiar – Livewire Images
http://www.livewireimages.com/SV/vidarbha/index.html

• Lie #8. (Food & Pesticide Corncobs) Brett Wilcox

• Lie #9. (Food Labeling Has Monsanto's Full Backing Screen Shot) *Monsanto.co.uk*,
http://www.monsanto.co.uk/highlights/ads/ad4.html
Note: The author captured a screenshot of the image found at this link on April 10, 2013. Monsanto has since replaced the image with a "redirect" to Monsanto UK's homepage.

• Lie #10 (GMO Tombstone) Brett Wilcox

- Lie #11 (Monsanto Man Pouring Roundup Over Earth) Brett & Brittany Wilcox
- Lie #12 ("We Need The Bees" Protester) Justin Zern
- Lie #13 (Corn Field, Foreclosure Sign) Brett Wilcox
- Lie #14 (Monsanto Men/Revolving Door) Madison & Brett Wilcox
- Lie #15 (Family Praying Over Roundup) Brett Wilcox
- Lie #16 (Baby Hand) Brett Wilcox
- Lie #17 (Lit Cigarette) Brett Wilcox
- Lie #18 (Donkey Head on Monsanto Man) Donkey Head © Depositphotos.com/FRANCISCO JAVIER HERRERO ISLA #12099738, Monsanto Man: Mikelann & Brett Wilcox
- Lie #19 (Monsanto Man As Satan) Brittany & Brett Wilcox
- Lie #20 (Donald Rumsfeld At Abu Ghraib) Secretary of Defense Donald H. Rumsfeld takes a tour of the Abu Ghraib Detention Center in Abu Ghraib, Iraq, on May 13, 2004. Rumsfeld and Chairman of the Joint Chiefs of Staff Gen. Richard B. Myers are in Iraq to visit the troops in Baghdad and Abu Ghraib.   DoD photo by Tech. Sgt. Jerry Morrison Jr., U.S. Air Force. (Released) http://www.defense.gov/photos/newsphoto.aspx?newsp hotoid=5089
- Lie #21 (Monsanto Man Drowning In Money) Brittany & Brett Wilcox
- Lie #22 (Dead Fish In Polluted River) © Depositphotos.com/Christian Draghici #11008588
- Lie #23 (Avoid Any Comments Screenshot, Underline Added) Brett Wilcox http://www.chemicalindustryarchives.org/search/pdfs/a nniston/19760925_257.pdf
- Lie #24 (Rowan The Butt Licking Dog) Annie Beechum

• Lie #25 (Fast Food Feast) © Depositphotos.com/Gennadiy Poznyakov #10526766

• Lie #26 (Pono Molokai Protesters) Justin Zern

• Lie #27 (Kauai Protesters) Justin Zern

• Lie #28 (Bank Vault Door) © Depositphotos.com/PILart #8438011

• Lie #29 (Wheat Field) Brett Wilcox

• Lie #30 (Confused Hiker) Brett Wilcox

• Lie #31 (Nuclear Blast) "Mushroom-shaped cloud and water column from the underwater Baker nuclear explosion of July 25, 1946. Photo taken from a tower on Bikini Island, 3.5 miles (5.6 km) away." http://en.wikipedia.org/wiki/Operation_Crossroads High res image at http://i.imgur.com/DgIEr0a.jpg

• Lie #32 (False FDA Statement) Brett Wilcox

• Lie #33 (Skull & Crossbones On Cereal) Brett Wilcox

• Lie #34 (Stanford University Employs Henry Miller) Jill Richardson. Digitally altered by Brett Wilcox

• Lie #35 (Nearly Empty Store Shelves) Brett Wilcox

• Lie #36 (No GMOs Prescription) Brett Wilcox

• Lie #37 (Man Holding Protest Sign) Alex GD

• Lie #38 (Monsanto Profits Before And After GMO Labels) Brett Wilcox

• Lie #39 (Monsanto Men Worshipping Monsanto Man On Golden Altar) Brett Wilcox

• Lie #40 (Plane Spraying Agent Orange) Vietnam War Photo Found On Internet

• Lie #41 ("Tumours in treated groups of rats in Prof. Gilles-Eric Séralini's 2012 study on GM maize and Roundup.") http://gmoseralini.org/portfolio-items/rat-tumors-gm-maize-and-roundup/

• Lie #42 (Before And After Monsanto Man) Brittany & Brett Wilcox

• Lie #43 ("A Farmer Plows His Field Before The Start Of The Sowing Season." 1/32)

Prashant Panjiar – Livewire Images

http://www.livewireimages.com/SV/vidarbha/index.html

• Lie #44 (Super M on Chest of Man In Suit) Brittany & Brett Wilcox

• Lie #45 (Screenshot of National Bioeconomy Blueprint) Brett Wilcox

"National Bioeconomy Blueprint," The White House, April 2012,

http://www.whitehouse.gov/sites/default/files/microsites/ostp/national_bioeconomy_blueprint_april_2012.pdf

• Lie #46 (Turkey) PC: © Depositphotos.com/José Manuel Gelpi Díaz #9438756

• Lie #47 ("Rama, the wife of Vijay Thamke, a farmer from Sonbardi village who committed suicide on 27 March, is consoled by her daughter Pooja." 8/32)

Prashant Panjiar – Livewire Images

http://www.livewireimages.com/SV/vidarbha/index.html

• Lie #48 (Cows Pooping On Monsanto Sign) Brett Wilcox

• Lie #49 (Roundup Spilling On Parched Ground) Brett Wilcox

• Lie #50 (Trust Us Mannequin) Brett Wilcox

Notes

Introduction

1. "A New Pledge for a New Company", Remarks by Hendrik A. Verfaillie, President and Chief Executive Officer, Monsanto Company, Farm Journal Conference, Washington, D.C., November 27, 2000, http://www.biotech-info.net/new_Monsanto.html

Lie #1: Monsanto Will Feed a Hungry World

1. Monsanto, http://www.monsanto.co.uk/highlights/ads/ad6.html

Quoted from a Monsanto ad distributed in Europe.

2. David Suzuki, Holly Dressel, *From Naked Ape to Super Species: A Personal Perspective on Humanity and the Global Ecocrisis*, Stoddart, 1999, p. 118

3. "Against the Grain," *Rachel's Environment and Health Weekly*, 637, February 11, 1999, see also Lappé and Bailey, Against the Grain, pp. 88-9

"Neither Monsanto nor any of the other genetic engineering companies appears to be developing genetically engineered crops that might solve global food shortages. Quite the opposite. If genetically engineered crops were aimed at feeding the hungry, then Monsanto and the others would be developing seeds with certain predictable characteristics: a) ability to grow on substandard or marginal soil; b) plants able to produce more high-quality protein with increased per-acre yield, without the need for expensive machinery, chemicals, fertilizers, or water; c) they would aim to favor small farms over larger farms; d) the seeds would be cheap and freely available without restrictive licensing; and e) they would be for crops that feed people, not meat animals. None of the genetically engineered crops now available, or in development (to the extent that these have been announced) has any of these desirable characteristics. Quite the opposite. The new genetically engineered seeds ... produce crops largely intended as feed for meat animals, not to provide protein for people. The genetic engineering revolution has nothing to do with feeding the world's hungry."

4. Luke Anderson, *Genetic Engineering, Food, and our Environment*, White River Junction, VT, Chelsea Green Publishing Company, 1999, pp. 55-57.

Lie #2: Monsanto Improves the Environment

1. *Monsanto*, http://www.monsanto.com/Pages/results.aspx?k=mission%20and%20pledge

2. *Greenpeace USA*, http://www.greenpeace.org/usa/en/campaigns/genetic-engineering/ge-industry/

"The transnational companies that produce genetically engineered (GE) food crops include several of the worst polluters of the 20th century. These "agbiotech" companies evolved from long-time chemical polluters that have reinvented themselves as "life sciences" companies. These companies see huge profits in controlling life patents, in denying consumers their right to know when food is genetically altered and in creating crops that require farmers to use the company's brand of pesticides."

3. Elizabeth Kucinich, "The Killing Fields: Industrial Agriculture, Dead Zones and Genetically Engineered Corn," *The Huffington Post*, August 1, 2013, http://www.huffingtonpost.com/elizabeth-kucinich/the-killing-fields-indust_b_3678515.html

4. Barbara L. Minton, "Monsanto: History of Contamination and Cover-up," *Natural News*, May 16, 2008, http://www.naturalnews.com/023254_Monsanto_PCB_toxic.html

Lie #3: Monsanto Respectfully Sues Farmers

1. "Monsanto's Commitment: Farmers and Patents," *Monsanto*, http://www.monsanto.com/newsviews/Pages/commitment-farmers-patents.aspx

2. "Monsanto vs. U.S. Farmers," *Center for Food Safety*, pp. 4-5, 36

http://www.centerforfoodsafety.org/pubs/CFSMOnsantovsFarmer
Report1.13.05.pdf

3. Chris Parker, "The Monsanto Menace," *Village Voice*, July 24,
2013, http://www.villagevoice.com/2013-07-24/restaurants/the-
monsanto-menace/full/

4. "Seed Giants vs. U.S. Farmers," *Center for Food Safety*, p. 1,
http://www.centerforfoodsafety.org/files/seed-
giants_final_04424.pdf

5. Marie-Monique Robin, "The World According To Monsanto:
Pollution, Corruption, and the Control of Our Food Supply, an
Investigation into the World's Most Controversial Company," (The
New Press, New York, 2010) p. 209

Lie #4: Monsanto Has Better Seeds

1. "Toxic Alert: Herbicide Now Detected in Human Urine,"
Mercola.com, October 23, 2012,
http://articles.mercola.com/sites/articles/archive/2012/10/23/glyp
hosate-found-in-human-urine.aspx

2. "University of Canterbury Researchers: GM is a Failing
Biotechnology," *Sustainable Pulse*, June 20, 2013,
http://sustainablepulse.com/2013/06/20/university-of-canterbury-
researchers-gm-is-a-failing-biotechnology/

3. "Analysis Finds Monsanto's GE Corn Nutritionally Inferior and
High in Toxins," *Mercola.com*, April 30, 2013,

http://articles.mercola.com/sites/articles/archive/2013/04/30/mo
nsanto-gmo-corn.aspx

4. "Seed Companies Owned By Monsanto," *Planet Infowars*,
December 26, 2012,
http://planet.infowars.com/uncategorized/seed-companies-
owned-by-monsanto

5. "Monocultures," *Carbon Trade Watch*,

http://www.carbontradewatch.org/issues/monoculture.html

6. "Tell the EPA You Want Lower, Not Higher, Limits on Monsanto's
Roundup!" *Organic Consumers Association*,

http://salsa3.salsalabs.com/o/50865/p/dia/action3/common/publi
c/?action_KEY=10886

7. Tom Laskawy, "Gut punch: Monsanto could be destroying your
microbiome," *Grist Magazine, Inc.*, May 23, 2010,
http://grist.org/food/gut-punch-monsanto-could-be-destroying-
your-microbiome/

8. John M. Pleasants, Karen S. Oberhauser, "Milkweed loss in
agricultural fields because of herbicide use: effect on the monarch
butterfly population," *Insect Conservation and Diversity*, Volume 6,
Issue 2, pages 135–144, March 2013,
http://onlinelibrary.wiley.com/doi/10.1111/j.1752-
4598.2012.00196.x/abstract?deniedAccessCustomisedMessage=&
userIsAuthenticated=false

9. "Monsanto Fails at Improving Agriculture," *Union of Concerned
Scientists*, http://www.ucsusa.org/food_and_agriculture/our-
failing-food-system/genetic-engineering/monsanto-fails-at-
improving.html

See also: "Decline of monarch butterflies overwintering in Mexico:
is the migratory phenomenon at risk?" *Insect Conservation and
Diversity* Volume 5, Issue 2 (March 2012): pp. 95-100. "Three
factors are implicated in the downward trend in the monarch's
abundance: (i) the loss of and reduction in quality of critical
overwintering habitat in Mexico through extensive illegal logging;
(ii) the widespread reduction of breeding habitat in the United
States due to continuing land development and the killing of the
monarch's principal larval foodplant, the common milkweed
Asclepias syriaca L. (Asclepiadaceae), because of increased use of
glyphosate herbicide to kill weeds growing in genetically
engineered, herbicide-resistant crops; and (iii) periodic extreme
weather conditions, such as those that occurred most recently in
2009, that decrease both the spring breeding in Texas and the
subsequent spring and summer breeding generations in the
eastern USA and southern Canada."

See also: Richard Conniff, "Tracking the Causes of Sharp Decline of
the Monarch Butterfly," *Yale University*, April 1, 2013,

http://e360.yale.edu/feature/tracking_the_causes_of_sharp__decl
ine_of_the_monarch_butterfly/2634/

Lie #5: 2013 World Food Prize Recipients Help Feed the World With GMOs

1. "World Food Prize Laureate Dr. Robert Fraley," *Monsanto*,
http://www.monsanto.com/improvingagriculture/Pages/world-
food-prize-laureate-dr-robert-fraley.aspx

2. "Three Scientists Win 27th Annual World Food Prize," *U.S.
Department of State*, June 19, 2013,
http://www.state.gov/r/pa/prs/ps/2013/06/210849.htm

3. John Kerry, Secretary of State, "Remarks at the World Food Prize
Laureate Announcement Ceremony," *U.S. Department of State*,
June 19, 2013,

http://www.state.gov/secretary/remarks/2013/06/210896.htm

4. Anthony Gucciardi, "Monsanto Exec Gets 'Nobel Peace Prize' of
Food," *Natural Society*, June 20, 2013,
http://naturalsociety.com/monsanto-exec-gets-nobel-peace-prize-
of-food/

5. "Sponsors," *The World Food Prize*,
http://www.worldfoodprize.org/en/about_the_prize/sponsors/

6. Frances Moore Lappé and Anna Lappé, "Choice of Monsanto
Betrays World Food Prize Purpose, Say Global Leaders," *The
Huffington Post*, June 26, 2013,
http://www.huffingtonpost.com/frances-moore-lappe-and-anna-
lappe/choice-of-monsanto-betray_b_3499045.html

Lie #6: Roundup Is Safe

1. Attorney General of the State of New York, Consumer Frauds
and Protection Bureau, Environmental Protection Bureau. 1996. In
the matter of Monsanto Company, respondent. Assurance of
discontinuance pursuant to executive law § 63(15). New York, NY,
Nov. False advertising by Monsanto regarding the safety of
Roundup herbicide (glyphosate).
http://www.mindfully.org/Pesticide/Monsanto-v-AGNYnov96.htm

2. "Monsanto Lies, Again (and Again and Again)," *Corporate Crime Daily*, October 17, 2009, http://corporatecrime.wordpress.com/2009/10/17/monsanto-lies-again-and-again-and-again/

"Monsanto has a long history of fraudulent statements about the safety of Roundup. In 1996, the New York Attorney General fined the company $50,000 for claims that Roundup was, you guessed it, biodegradable and good for the environment."

3. "Monsanto guilty in 'false ad' row," *BBC News*, http://news.bbc.co.uk/2/hi/europe/8308903.stm

"The court confirmed an earlier judgment that Monsanto had falsely advertised its herbicide as "biodegradable" and claimed it "left the soil clean".

The company was fined 15,000 euros (£13,800; $22,400). It has yet to comment on the judgment.

Roundup is the world's best-selling herbicide.

Monsanto also sells crops genetically-engineered to be tolerant to Roundup.

French environmental groups had brought the case in 2001 on the basis that glyphosate, Roundup's main ingredient, is classed as "dangerous for the environment" by the European Union.

In the latest ruling, France's Supreme Court upheld two earlier convictions against Monsanto by the Lyon criminal court in 2007, and the Lyon court of appeal in 2008, the AFP news agency reports."

4. "R.E.D. Facts: Glyphosate," *Environmental Protection Agency*, http://www.epa.gov/oppsrrd1/REDs/factsheets/0178fact.pdf

5. "Roundup more toxic than officially declared - new study," *GMWatch*, February 21, 2013, http://www.gmwatch.org/latest-listing/52-2013/14654-roundup-more-toxic-than-officially-declared-new-study

"In a new research published in the highly ranked scientific journal Toxicology, Robin Mesnage, Benoit Bernay and Professor Gilles-Eric

Seralini, from the University of Caen, France, have proven (from a study of nine Roundup-like herbicides) that the most toxic compound is not glyphosate, which is the substance the most assessed by regulatory authorities, but a compound that is not always listed on the label, called POE-15."

6. "List of References on the Health Effects of Glyphosate (Roundup)," *Institute For Responsible Technology*, http://responsibletechnology.org/gmo-dangers/health-risks/reference-health-effects-of-glyphosate

7. Anthony Samsel, Stephanie Seneff, Glyphosate's Suppression of Cytochrome P450 Enzymes and Amino Acid Biosynthesis by the Gut Microbiome: Pathways to Modern Diseases, *Entropy*, Volume 15, Issue 4, 1416-1463, April 18, 2013, http://www.mdpi.com/1099-4300/15/4/1416

8. "Roundup: 'The ultimate killing machine'," *GMOSeralini*, http://gmoseralini.org/roundup-the-ultimate-killing-machine/

"Roundup is marketed to the public as a safe herbicide, often with claims that it's biodegradable or can be used safely around pets and children. Ironically it's also marketed to farmers as 'the ultimate killing machine' (see video above)!"

9. "Monsanto's Roundup Herbicide—Featuring the Darth Vader Chemical," *YouTube Channel: GeneticRoulette*, May 10, 2013, http://www.youtube.com/watch?v=h_AHLDXF5aw

Lie #7: Bt Cotton Improves Indian Farmers' Lives

1. Coordinated by Navdanya and Navdanya International, the International Commission on the Future of Food and Agriculture, with the participation of The Center for Food Safety (CFS), *The GM Emperor Has No Clothes: A Global Citizens Report on the State of GMOs – False Promises, Failed Technologies*, p. 29, http://image.guardian.co.uk/sys-files/Environment/documents/2011/10/19/GMOEMPEROR.pdf

"In India, Monsanto's advertising slogan is: 'India delights as cotton farmers' lives transform for the better.' But the widows of the more than 250,000 farmer suicides in India related to GM cotton crop failures are certainly not delighting."

2. Coordinated by Navdanya and Navdanya International, the International Commission on the Future of Food and Agriculture, with the participation of The Center for Food Safety (CFS), *The GM Emperor Has No Clothes: A Global Citizens*

Report on the State of GMOs – False Promises, Failed Technologies, pp. 21, 25 29, 30, 41, 42, http://image.guardian.co.uk/sys-files/Environment/documents/2011/10/19/GMOEMPEROR.pdf

3. "GMO A Go Go - Truth about GMOs explained in new animated cartoon," *NaturalNews.com*, http://www.youtube.com/watch?v=KGqQV6ObFCQ

4. "Farmer Suicides in India – Is There a Connection with Bt Cotton?" *Monsanto*, http://www.monsanto.com/newsviews/Pages/india-farmer-suicides.aspx

5. Dr. Vandana Shiva, "The Seeds Of Suicide: How Monsanto Destroys Farming," *Global Research*, June 24, 2013, http://www.globalresearch.ca/the-seeds-of-suicide-how-monsanto-destroys-farming/5329947

Lie #8: Substantial Equivalence

1. "Food Safety," *Monsanto*, http://www.monsanto.com/newsviews/Pages/food-safety.aspx

2. Ms. Samm Simpson, Exposing the GMO Lynchpin, Institute For Responsible Technology, http://www.responsibletechnology.org/posts/exposing-the-gmo-lynchpin/

3. E. Millstone, E. Brunner, S. Mayer, "Beyond 'substantial equivalence'". Nature. 1999; 401(6753): 525–526, http://planete.blogs.nouvelobs.com/media/02/02/453972038.pdf

4. "GMO Dangers," *Institute For Responsible Technology*, http://www.responsibletechnology.org/gmo-dangers

5. Jeffrey Smith, State-Of-The-Science On The Health Risks Of GM Foods, Institute For Responsible Technology, January 24, 2013,

http://www.responsibletechnology.org/posts/wp-content/uploads/2013/01/State-of-the-Science-of-GMO-Health-Risks-sm-.2013.pdf

6. Janie Boschma, "Monsanto: Big Guy on the Block When it Comes to Friends in Washington," *OpenSecrets.org*, February 19, 2013, http://www.opensecrets.org/news/2013/02/monsanto.html

7. Mae-Wan Ho, Ph.D and Lim Li Ching, *GMO Free: Exposing the Hazards of Biotechnology to Ensure the Integrity of Our Food Supply*, Ridgefield, CT, Vital Health Publishing, 2004, p. 16, http://www.amazon.com/GMO-Free-Mae-Wan-Ho/dp/1890612375/

8. Sayer Ji, "Extreme Toxicity of Roundup Destroys GM/Non-GM 'Substantial Equivalence' Argument," *GreenMedInfo*, June 23, 2013, http://www.greenmedinfo.com/blog/monsantos-game-over-extreme-toxicity-roundup-destroys-justification-gm

9. Carla L Barberis, Cecilia S Carranza, Stella M Chiacchiera, Carina E Magnoli, "Influence of herbicide glyphosate on growth and aflatoxin B1 production by Aspergillus section Flavi strains isolated from soil on in vitro assay," *J Environ Sci Health B.* 2013 ;48(12):1070-9. PMID: 24007484

10. Sayer Ji, "BREAKING: Study Links Roundup 'Weedkiller' To Overgrowth of Deadly Fungal Toxins - Page 2," *GreenMedInfo*, September 9, 2013, http://www.greenmedinfo.com/blog/breaking-study-links-roundup-weedkiller-overgrowth-deadly-fungal-toxins-1?page=2

Lie #9: Food Labeling Has Monsanto's Full Backing

1. "Food Labeling. It Has Monsanto's Full Backing," *Monsanto.co.uk*, http://www.monsanto.co.uk/highlights/ads/ad4.html

Note: I captured a screenshot of the image found at this link on April 10, 2013. Monsanto has since replaced the image with a "redirect" to Monsanto UK's homepage.

2. Stacy Malkan, "Monsanto promotes GMO labeling in Europe; yet spends millions to fight it in California," *carighttoknow.org*,

September 4, 2012, http://www.carighttoknow.org/monsanto_ads

3. Lynn Waddell, Weekly Planet Staff Writer, *Don't Have a Cow. BGH is the story behind the story. What exactly is it and should we be alarmed?* http://www.foxbghsuit.com/wp02.htm

4. "Labeling Issues, Revolving Doors, rBGH, Bribery and Monsanto," *SourceWatch*, http://www.sourcewatch.org/index.php/Labeling_Issues,_Revolving_Doors,_rBGH,_Bribery_and_Monsanto

5. "The Mystery of Monsanto's Ever-Changing Stance on GMO Labeling," *Get Real: Taste The Truth*, http://www.getrealmaple.com/the-trouble-with-table-syrup/monsanto-gmo-labeling.php

6. *Monsanto*, http://www.monsanto.com/newsviews/Pages/food-labeling.aspx

Lie #10: GMOs Are Safe

1. "Food Safety," *Monsanto*, http://www.monsanto.com/newsviews/Pages/food-safety.aspx

2. John Robbins, *The Food Revolution*, Conari Press, York Beach, ME, 2001, p. 333.

3. Michael Antoniou, Claire Robinson, John Fagan, "GMO Myths and Truths," *earthopensource*, June, 2012, p. 49 http://earthopensource.org/files/pdfs/GMO_Myths_and_Truths/GMO_Myths_and_Truths_1.3b.pdf

4. Michael Ravensthorpe, "Patent confirms that aspartame is the excrement of GM bacteria," *Natural News*, August 24, http://www.naturalnews.com/041766_aspartame_gm_bacteria_patent.html

5. Jeffrey M. Smith, *Seeds of Deception: Exposing Industry and Government Lies About the Safety of the Genetically Engineered Foods You're Eating*, Yes! Books, Fairfield, Iowa, 2003, p. 101

6. "IGF-1 As One-Stop Cancer Shop," *NutritionFacts.org*, http://nutritionfacts.org/video/igf-1-as-one-stop-cancer-shop/

7. Trevor Wells, "Monsanto tells pack of lies in South Africa,"

Mathaba, June 27, 2007,
http://www.mathaba.net/news/?x=556517

8. "SOMETHING SMELLS, AND IT'S NOT THE PIGS,"
Monsantoblog.com, June 13, 2013,
http://monsantoblog.com/2013/06/13/something-smells-and-its-
not-the-pigs/

9. "Now Playing: Genetically Modified Foods: Are They Safe? Pt 2"
The Dr. Oz Show, http://www.doctoroz.com/episode/gmo-foods-
are-they-dangerous-your-health?video=15169

10. "Agent Orange Victims Sue Monsanto," *CorpWatch*,
http://www.corpwatch.org/article.php?id=11638

11. Richard Schiffman, "Dow and Monsanto's Plan to Increase the
Toxic Pesticides Sprayed in America's Heartland," *The Huffington
Post*, February 17, 2012, http://www.huffingtonpost.com/richard-
schiffman/dow-and-monsanto-team-up-_b_1256725.html

12. "Agent Orange Ready Corn," *Food & Water Watch*,
http://www.foodandwaterwatch.org/food/genetically-engineered-
foods/24-d-corn/

13. Janine Cohen and Karen Michelmore, "Chemical Time Bomb,"
Australian Broadcasting Corporation, July 23, 2013,
http://www.abc.net.au/4corners/stories/2013/07/22/3806111.htm

Lie #11: GMOs Reduce Pesticide Use

1. "A New Pledge for a New Company," Remarks by Hendrik A.
Verfaillie, President and Chief Executive Officer, Monsanto
Company, Farm Journal Conference, Washington, D.C., November
27, 2000, http://www.biotech-info.net/new_Monsanto.html

2. Charles Benbrook, Ph.D., *Impacts of Genetically Engineered
Crops on Pesticide Use: The First Thirteen Years*, November, 2009,
The Organic Center, www.organic-center.org, http://www.organic-
center.org/science.pest.php?action=view&report_id=159

3. Jim Riddle, "GM Crops Pose Problems," *AgriNews*,
https://www.facebook.com/RightToKnowMN/posts/30146651998
2943, Posted by Right to Know Minnesota on March 9, 2013

4. "The Garden Island: Shiva brings anti-GMO message to Kaua'i," *Occupy Monsanto*, http://occupy-monsanto.com/the-garden-island-shiva-brings-anti-gmo-message-to-kauai/

Lie #12: Monsanto Promotes Honey Bee Health

1. "Monsanto Company Forms Honey Bee Advisory Council, Pledges Support For Honey Bee Health At First-Of-Its-Kind Summit, *Monsanto*, June 13, 2013, http://monsanto.mediaroom.com/2013-06-13-monsanto-company-forms-honey-bee-advisory-council-pledges-support-for-honey-bee-health-at-first-of-its-kind-summit

2. "The Buzz on Beeologics," *Monsanto*, http://www.monsanto.com/newsviews/Pages/the-buzz-on-beologics.aspx

3. "Blamed for Bee Collapse, Monsanto Buys Leading Bee Research Firm," *Natural Society*, http://naturalsociety.com/monsanto-bee-collapse-buys-bee-research-firm/

4. "Permanent Peoples' Tribunal, Session on Agrochemical Transnational Corporations," December 3-6, 2001, http://agricorporateaccountability.net/sites/default/files/tpp_bang alore3dec2011.pdf

5. "Controversial Agrichemical Company Monsanto Holds Bee Health Conference," *Nature World News*, June 17, 2013, http://www.natureworldnews.com/articles/2498/20130617/contr oversial-agrichemical-company-monsanto-holds-bee-health.htm

6. Bryan, Walsh, "The Plight of the Honeybee," Time Magazine, August 19, 2013, p. 31

Lie #13: Monsanto Improves Farmers' Lives

1. "Products: What We Do," *Monsanto*, http://www.monsanto.com/products/Pages/default.aspx

2. *Plants For a Future,* http://www.pfaf.org/user/default.aspx

"There are over 20,000 species of edible plants in the world yet fewer than 20 species now provide 90% of our food. Large areas of land devoted to single crops increase dependence upon intervention of chemicals and intensive control methods with the added threat of chemical resistant insects and new diseases. The changing world climate greatly affecting cultivation indicates a greater diversity is needed."

3. Fritz Kreiss, "We Used To Have 307 Kinds Of Corn. Guess How Many Are Left?" *Occupy Monsanto*, April 19, 2012, http://www.occupymonsanto360.org/2012/04/19/we-used-to-have-307-kinds-of-corn-guess-how-many-are-left/

4. "EPA's Regulation of Bacillus thuringiensis (Bt) Crops," *Environmental Protection Agency*, May, 2002, http://www.epa.gov/oppbppd1/biopesticides/pips/regofbtcrops.htm

5. Tom Philpott, "Do GMO Crops Really Have Higher Yields?" *Mother Jones*, February 13, 2013, http://www.motherjones.com/tom-philpott/2013/02/do-gmo-crops-have-lower-yields

6. Fritz Kreiss, "Monsanto 'Owned' Heirloom Seednames," *Occupy Monsanto*, March 17, 2012, http://www.occupymonsanto360.org/2012/03/17/monsanto-owned-seednames/

7. E. Freeman, "Farmers Reporting Farmers - Part 2," *Monsanto*, October 10, 2008, http://www.monsanto.com/newsviews/Pages/Farmers-Reporting-Farmers-Part-2.aspx

8. Daniel Klein, "Perennial Plate in India: GMOs and Farmer Suicides [VIDEO]," *Civil Eats*, February 19, 2013, http://civileats.com/2013/02/19/perennial-plate-in-india-gmos-and-farmer-suicides/

9. *Greenpeace USA*, http://www.greenpeace.org/usa/en/campaigns/genetic-engineering/ge-industry/ "The transnational companies that produce genetically engineered (GE) food crops include several of the worst polluters of the 20th century. These "agbiotech" companies evolved from long-time chemical polluters that have reinvented themselves as "life sciences" companies. These companies see huge profits in controlling life patents, in denying consumers their right to know when food is genetically altered and

in creating crops that require farmers to use the company's brand of pesticides."

10. Carey Gillam, "Monsanto Lawsuit: Organic Farmers Appeal U.S. District Court Decision," *The Huffington Post*, March 28, 2012, http://www.huffingtonpost.com/2012/03/28/monsanto-lawsuit-organic-farmers-appeal_n_1385693.html

11. Wayne Barrett, "Mitt Romney, Monsanto Man, *The Nation*, September 12, 2012, http://www.thenation.com/article/169885/mitt-romney-monsanto-man#

12. Anthony Gucciardi, "5 Million Farmers Sue Monsanto for $7.7 Billion," *Infowars*, June 5, 2012, http://www.infowars.com/5-million-farmers-sue-monsanto-for-7-7-billion/

Lie #14: No Revolving Door

1. "Food, Inc. Movie," *Monsanto*, http://www.monsanto.com/food-inc/Pages/default.aspx

2. "Monsanto, the Government, Monopoly Claims," *Monsanto*, http://www.monsanto.com/food-inc/Pages/monsanto-revolving-door.aspx

3. Janie Boschma, "Monsanto: Big Guy on the Block When it Comes to Friends in Washington," *OpenSecrets.org*, February 19, 2013, http://www.opensecrets.org/news/2013/02/monsanto.html

4. "Corporatism Wins, Again: SCOTUS Unanimously rules in favor of Monsanto, vs an Indiana Farmer!" *The Daily Paul*, May 13, 2013, http://www.dailypaul.com/285352/alert-corporatism-wins-again-scotus-unanimously-rules-in-favor-of-monsanto-vs-indiana-farmer

5. Dr. Mercola, "Banned in Germany, But You're Probably Still Eating It," *Mercola.com*, January 31, 2012, http://articles.mercola.com/sites/articles/archive/2012/01/31/monsanto-worst-company-of-2011.aspx

Lie #15: GMOs Reduce Herbicide Use

1. "Practical Approaches to Managing Weeds," *Monsanto*, http://www.monsanto.com/weedmanagement/Pages/default.aspx

2. N.L. Swanson, "Genetically Modified Organisms and the deterioration of health in the United States, *Sustainable Pulse*, April 24, 2013, http://sustainablepulse.com/wp-content/uploads/GMO-health.pdf, "This document was first published as a series of articles on Seattle examiner.com."

3. Jim Riddle, "GM Crops Pose Problems," *AgriNews*, https://www.facebook.com/RightToKnowMN/posts/30146651998 2943, Posted by Right to Know Minnesota on March 9, 2013

4. "Glyphosate-resistant weed problem extends to more species, more farms," *Farm Industry News*, January 29, 2013. http://farmindustrynews.com/herbicides/glyphosate-resistant-weed-problemextends-more-species-more-farms

5. "From Super Weeds to Super Bugs...Thanks Monsanto!" http://www.youtube.com/watch?v=Q9z4VjznPO4

6. Tom Laskawy, "First came superweeds; now come the superbugs!" *Grist Magazine, Inc.*, http://grist.org/article/first-came-superweeds-and-now-come-the-superbugs/

7. "GMO Myths and Truths Report," *Earth Open Source*, http://earthopensource.org/index.php/5-gm-crops-impacts-on-the-farm-and-environment/5-2-myth-gm-crops-decrease-pesticide-use

Lie #16: Glyphosate Does Not Cause Birth Defects

1. "Argentina's Bad Seeds," *Aljazeera*, http://www.aljazeera.com/programmes/peopleandpower/2013/0 3/201331313434142322.html

2. "June 2011 Earth Open Source report on Roundup 6/8/2011," *Monsanto*, http://www.monsanto.com/newsviews/Pages/June-2011-earth-open-source-report-on-roundup.aspx

3. Paganelli, A., Gnazzo, V., Acosta, H., López, S.L., Carrasco, A.E. 2010. Glyphosate-based herbicides produce teratogenic effects on vertebrates by impairing retinoic acid signalling. Chem. Res. Toxicol., August, http://pubs.acs.org/doi/abs/10.1021/tx1001749

4. Michael Antoniou, Mohamed Ezz El-Din Mostafa Habib, C. Vyvyan Howard, Richard C. Jennings, Carlo Leifert, Rubens Onofre

Nodari, Claire Robinson, John Fagan, "Roundup and birth defects: Is the public being kept in the dark?" *Earth Open Source*, June, 2011, p. 5-6, http://earthopensource.org/files/pdfs/Roundup-and-birth-defects/RoundupandBirthDefectsv5.pdf

Lie #17: Monsanto Science is Solid

1. "A New Pledge for a New Company," Remarks by Hendrik A. Verfaillie, President and Chief Executive Officer, Monsanto Company, Farm Journal Conference, Washington, D.C., November 27, 2000, http://www.biotech-info.net/new_Monsanto.html

2. JL Domingo, "Health risks of GM foods: Many opinions but few data," *Science*, 2000; 288(5472): 1748–1749.31, p. 25, http://www.nongmoproject.org/wp-content/uploads/2010/08/GMO_Myths_and_Truths_1.31.pdf

3. "Monsanto Code of Business Conduct," *Monsanto*, p. 1, http://www.monsanto.com/SiteCollectionDocuments/Code-of-Business-Conduct-PDFs/code_of_conduct_english.pdf

4. "MONSANTO KNEW ABOUT PCB TOXICITY FOR DECADES," *Chemical Industry Archives*, http://www.chemicalindustryarchives.org/dirtysecrets/annistonind epth/toxicity.asp

5. "Agent Orange Victims Sue Monsanto," *CorpWatch*, http://www.corpwatch.org/article.php?id=11638

6. Michael Antoniou, Claire Robinson, John Fagan, "GMO Myths and Truths: An evidence-based examination of the claims made for the safety and efficacy of genetically modified crops," *Earth Open Source*, June 2012, p. 46, http://www.nongmoproject.org/wp-content/uploads/2010/08/GMO_Myths_and_Truths_1.31.pdf

7. Andrea Baillie, "Suzuki Warns of Frankenstein Foods," CP Wire, October 18, 1999

8. Dave Murphy, "The March to Stop Monsanto: Taking Back Our Food, Our Farms, Our Democracy and Our Planet," *The Huffington Post*, May 28, 2013, http://www.huffingtonpost.com/dave-murphy/monsanto-gmo-food_b_3337043.html

9. Jeffrey M. Smith, *Genetic Roulette: The Gamble of Our Lives* (DVD

Documentary), 2012, http://geneticroulettemovie.com/

Lie #18: We Can Assume GMOs Are Safe

1. K. Sauer, "How We Establish Biotech Crop Safety: Product Safety for Food and Feed," *Monsanto*, March 30, 2009, http://www.monsanto.com/newsviews/Pages/Biotech-Food-GMO-Safety.aspx

2. "Biotech's Dirty Tricks Exposed in New Documentary Scientists Under Attack," *Institute for Responsible Technology*, http://www.responsibletechnology.org/posts/biotech's-dirty-tricks-exposed-in-new-documentary-scientists-under-attack/

3. Barbara Keeler and Marc Lappé, "Some Food for FDA Regulation," Los Angeles Times, January 7, 2001

4. Sheldon Rampton and John Stauber, *Trust Us We're Experts*, New York, New York: Jeremy P. Tarcher/ Putnam, 2001, p. 154

5. Jeffrey M. Smith, *Seeds of Deception*, Fairfield, IA, Yes! Books, 2003 pp. 34-38.

6. "Doctors Warn: Avoid Genetically Modified Food," *Institute for Responsible Technology*, http://www.responsibletechnology.org/doctors-warn

7. "Biotech Propaganda Cooks Dangers out of GM Potatoes," *Institute for Responsible Technology*, http://www.responsibletechnology.org/posts/biotech-propaganda-cooks-dangers-out-of-gm-potatoes-2/

8. "Genetically Modified Foods," *American Academy of Environmental Medicine*, www.aaemonline.org/gmopost.html

9. Michael Antoniou, Claire Robinson, John Fagan, "GMO Myths and Truths," *earthopensource*, June, 2012, p. 48 http://earthopensource.org/files/pdfs/GMO_Myths_and_Truths/GMO_Myths_and_Truths_1.3b.pdf

10. "65 Health Risks of GM Foods," *Institute For Responsible Technology*, http://responsibletechnology.org/gmo-dangers/65-health-risks/1notes, "Eyewitness reports: Animals avoid GMOs. 1. When given a choice, several animals avoided eating GM food. 2. In

farmer-run tests, cows and pigs repeatedly passed up GM corn. 3. Animals that avoided GM food include cows, pigs, geese, squirrels, elk, deer, raccoons, mice and rats."

11. "Activist Investor to Challenge Monsanto CEO to be More Transparent at January 31 Annual Shareholder Meeting," *Occupy Monsanto*, January 31, 2013, http://occupy-monsanto.com/press-release-for-the-monsanto-annual-shareholder-meeting/

Lie #19: GMO Opponents Are Anti-Science

1. Johan Bakker, "Some Straight Talk About GMOs - Interview With Professor Philip Stott, *Agriculture Online*, July 3, 2000, http://www.monsanto.co.uk/news/2000/july2000/03072000agriconline.html

2. Yves, Smith, "Revealed: World's Most Predatory Company is Poisoning You, New Study finds 'severe toxic effects' of commonly used Monsanto herbicides, *AlterNet*, September 20, 2012, http://www.alternet.org/food/revealed-worlds-most-predatory-company-poisoning-you

3. Grace Kiser, "The 12 Least Ethical Companies In The World: Covalence's Ranking (PHOTOS, POLL)," *The Huffington Post*, First Posted: March 30, 2010, Updated: May, 25, 2011, http://www.huffingtonpost.com/2010/01/28/the-least-ethical-compani_n_440073.html

4. John Vidal, environmental editor, "The wasteland: how years of secret chemical dumping left a toxic legacy: Monsanto helped to create one of the most contaminated sites in Britain," *The Guardian*, February 11, 2007, http://www.guardian.co.uk/environment/2007/feb/12/uknews.pollution1

5. Kristine Lofgren, "Monsanto Has Sued Hundreds of Small Farmers, Heads to the Supreme Court," *Inhabitat.com*, February 13, 2013, http://inhabitat.com/monsanto-has-sued-hundreds-of-small-farmers-heads-to-the-supreme-court/

6. "Monsanto Facilities Round The World," *Monsanto*, http://www.monsanto.com/whoweare/Pages/our-locations.aspx

7. "Just Label It!," http://justlabelit.org/

"Most Americans haven't been told about some of the ingredients that are in the food they eat. So it's no wonder that 92% of Americans want to label genetically engineered foods."

8. La Via Campesina, Friends of the Earth International, Combat Monsanto, "Combatting Monsanto: Grassroots resistance to the corporate power of agribusiness in the era of the 'green economy' and a changing climate," *Friends of the Earth International*, April 4, 2012, http://www.foei.org/en/resources/publications/pdfs/2012/combat ting-monsanto/

9. "Secrecy and Spoiler studies -- the Monsanto method," *GM-Free Cmyru*, http://www.gmfreecymru.org/documents/secrecyandspoiler.html

10. Claire Robinson, MPhil, "Don't Look, Don't Find: Health Hazards of Genetically Modified Food," *GMO Seralini*, Spring 2013, http://gmoseralini.org/wp-content/uploads/2013/04/GM_Food.pdf

This article is "A new peer-reviewed article has been published on the health hazards of genetically modified foods in Vital Link, the journal of the Canadian Association of Naturopathic Doctors. The article was commissioned by the journal and was written by Claire Robinson, managing editor of GMO Seralini, GMWatch editor and research director of Earth Open Source." http://gmoseralini.org/dont-look-dont-find-health-hazards-of-genetically-modified-food/

11. "Seralini Backs US Organizations in GMO Labeling Fight," *Sustainable Pulse*, April 4, 2013, http://sustainablepulse.com/2013/04/04/seralini-backs-us-organizations-in-gmo-labeling-fight/

12. F. William Engdahl, "GMO Scandal: The Long Term Effects of Genetically Modified Food on Humans," *Global Research*, January 22, 2013 and July 29, 2009, http://www.globalresearch.ca/gmo-scandal-the-long-term-effects-of-genetically-modified-food-on-humans/14570

13. "35 individuals who worked for Monsanto and the U.S. Government," *Occupy Monsanto*, March 3, 2012, http://occupy-monsanto.com/35-individuals-who-worked-for-monsanto-andthe-u-s-government/

14. "Monsanto's latest acquisition settles bribery charges," *GMWatch*, July 28, 2007, http://www.gmwatch.org/latest-listing/46-2007/1095-monsantos-latest-acquisition-settles-bribery-charges-2872007

15. "Lobbying and Advertising," *Union of Concerned Scientists*, http://www.ucsusa.org/food_and_agriculture/our-failing-food-system/genetic-engineering/lobbying-and-advertising.html

16. Wayne Barrett, "Mitt Romney, Monsanto Man, *The Nation*, September 12, 2012, http://www.thenation.com/article/169885/mitt-romney-monsanto-man#

17. Daisy Luther, "Sen. Roy Blunt: Monsanto's Congressional Judas," *The Organic Pepper*, March 28, 2013, http://www.theorganicprepper.ca/sen-roy-blunt-monsantos-congressional-judas-03282013

18. Ocean Robbins, "Did Monsanto Trick California Voters?" *The Huffington Post*, http://www.huffingtonpost.com/ocean-robbins/monsanto-prop-37_b_2088934.html

19. Jeffrey Smith, "Monsanto Forced Fox TV to Censor Coverage of Dangerous Milk Drug," *The Huffington Post*, http://www.huffingtonpost.com/jeffrey-smith/monsanto-forced-fox-tv-to_b_186428.html

20. Anthony Gucciardi, "US to Start 'Trade Wars' with Nations Opposed to Monsanto, GMO Crops," *Natural Society*, January 3, 2012, http://naturalsociety.com/us-start-trade-wars-with-nations-opposed-to-monsanto-gmo-crops

21. Nancy Scola, "Why Iraqi Farmers Might Prefer Death to Paul Bremer's Order 81" *AlterNet*, September 18, 2007, http://www.alternet.org/story/62273/why_iraqi_farmers_might_prefer_death_to_paul_bremer's_order_81

Lie #20: Seeds of Democracy in Iraq

1. F. William Engdahl, "Iraq and Washington's 'seeds of democracy'," *Current Concerns*, July 30, 2005, http://www.currentconcerns.ch/archive/2005/05/20050507.php

2. Robbie Gennet, "Donald Rumsfeld and the Strange History of Aspartame," *The Huffington Post*, January 6, 2011, http://www.huffingtonpost.com/robbie-gennet/donald-rumsfeld-and-the-s_b_805581.html

3. Michael Ravensthorpe, "Patent confirms that aspartame is the excrement of GM bacteria," *Natural News*, August 24, http://www.naturalnews.com/041766_aspartame_gm_bacteria_patent.html

4. Vandana Shiva, "GM Seeds and the Militarization of Food – and Everything Else," *Seed Freedom*, http://seedfreedom.in/gm-seeds-and-the-militarization-of-food-and-everything-else/

Lie #21: Monsanto Can't Afford to Lose One Dollar of Business

1. "Pollution Letter," *Monsanto*, February 16, 1970, full memo posted at Chemical Industry Archives website, http://www.chemicalindustryarchives.org/search/pdfs/anniston/19700216_205.pdf

2. "Monsanto Lies, Again (and Again and Again)," *Corporate Crime Daily*, October 17, 2009, http://corporatecrime.wordpress.com/2009/10/17/monsanto-lies-again-and-again-and-again/

Lie #22: Monsanto Acted Responsibly with PCBs

1. [Trial Transcript, Owens v. Monsanto CV-96-J-440-E, (N.D. Alabama April 4, 2001), pg. 454, line 6] Quoted from http://www.chemicalindustryarchives.org/dirtysecrets/annistonindepth/toxicity.asp

2. "Conspiracy of Silence: The story of how three corporate giants -- Monsanto , GE and Westinghouse -- covered their toxic trail," *Sierra*, http://www.sierraclub.org/sierra/200103/conspiracy.asp

3. "Letters From GE and Monsanto," *Planet Waves*, Statement made by M. A. Pierle, Vice-President, Environment, Safety and Health, Monsanto Company, St. Louis, Missouri, http://www.planetwaves.net/response.html

4. "MONSANTO KNEW ABOUT PCB TOXICITY FOR DECADES," *Environmental Working Group*, http://www.chemicalindustryarchives.org/dirtysecrets/annistonindepth/toxicity.asp

5. "PCB Check Set For New York City Schools," *News Inferno*, http://www.newsinferno.com/?p=26847

6. "Toxic Contamination in The Arctic," *BlueVoice.org*, http://www.bluevoice.org/news_toxicarctic.php

7. "EarthTalk: Toxic dead beached whales?" *YubaNet.com*, http://yubanet.com/opinions/EarthTalk-Toxic-dead-beached-whales_printer.php

8. "Food Sources of PCB Chemical Pollutants," *NutritionFacts.org*, http://nutritionfacts.org/video/food-sources-of-pcb-chemical-pollutants/

Lie #23: Monsanto is Not Liable

1. D.R. Bishop, D. Wood, "PCB Preparedness Q & A," *Monsanto*, September 29, 1976, http://www.chemicalindustryarchives.org/search/pdfs/anniston/19760925_257.pdf

2. "Monsanto's Roundup Herbicide—Featuring the Darth Vader Chemical," *Institute For Responsible Technology*, http://action.responsibletechnology.org/p/salsa/web/common/public/content?content_item_KEY=11129

Lie #24: GMOs Are Safe for Animals

1. "Animal Performance Assessments" *Monsanto*, http://www.monsanto.com/products/Pages/animal-safety-assessment.aspx

2. "Genetically Modified Foods," *American Academy of Environmental Medicine*,

http://www.aaemonline.org/gmopost.html

3. "Genetically Modified Soy Linked to Sterility, Infant Mortality," *Institute for Responsible Technology*, http://www.responsibletechnology.org/article-gmo-soy-linked-to-sterility

4. Jeffrey M. Smith, *Seeds of Deception: Exposing Industry and Government Lies About the Safety of the Genetically Engineered Foods You're Eating*, Yes! Books, Fairfield, Iowa, 2003, p. 157

5. "65 Health Risks of GM Foods," *Monsanto*, http://www.responsibletechnology.org/gmo-dangers/65-health-risks/1notes

6. "10 Reasons to Avoid GMOs," *Institute For Responsible Technology*, http://www.responsibletechnology.org/10-Reasons-to-Avoid-GMOs

7. "Food Safety," *Monsanto*, http://www.monsanto.com/newsviews/Pages/food-safety.aspx

8. Steven M. Druker, JD, "Biodeception, How the Food and Drug Administration Is Misrepresenting the Facts About Risks of Genetically Engineered Foods and Violating the Laws Meant to Regulate Them," Alliance For Bio-Integrity, http://www.biointegrity.org/FDADeception.html

Lie #25: GMOs Provide Truly Remarkable Benefits

1. "A New Pledge for a New Company," Remarks by Hendrik A. Verfaillie, President and Chief Executive Officer, Monsanto Company, Farm Journal Conference, Washington, D.C., November 27, 2000 http://www.biotech-info.net/new_Monsanto.html

2. Andrew Kimbrell, *Your Right to Know: Genetic Engineering and the Secret Changes in Your Food*, Earth Aware, San Rafael, California, 2007

3. Quoted from "Biotech's Dirty Tricks Exposed in New Documentary Scientists Under Attack," *Institute for Responsible Technology*, http://www.responsibletechnology.org/posts/biotech's-dirty-tricks-exposed-in-new-documentary-scientists-under-attack/

4. Adrian Ewins, "Biotech must cater to consumers, says expert," *The Western Producer*, April 4, 2002, http://www.producer.com/2002/04/biotech-must-cater-to-consumers-says-expert/

Lie #26: Hawaiians Who Oppose Monsanto and Gang Are Not Pono

1. The Maui News (Page A-7) April 14, 2013, Posted on Facebook by Save Hawaii From Monsanto, https://www.facebook.com/photo.php?fbid=505643512829122&set=a.486365454756928.108097.486359274757546&type=1&theater

2. Facebook group: Save Hawaii From Monsanto, https://www.facebook.com/Save.Hawai.from.Monsanto?group_id=0

3. Imani Altemus-Williams, "The struggle to reclaim paradise," *Waging Nonviolence*, April 10, 2013, http://wagingnonviolence.org/feature/the-struggle-to-reclaim-paradise/

4. Pattye Kealohalani Wright, "The Meaning of Being 'PONO'," *RealHula.com*, http://www.realhula.com/kumuWis-PONO.html

Lie #27: The World Has Largely Embraced GMOs

1. "Does Monsanto Have Undue Influence on Governments?" *Monsanto*, http://www.monsanto.com/newsviews/Pages/revolving-door.aspx

2. Merlyn Seeley, "March Against Monsanto Worldwide Event Makes History," Gateway Green Alliance: Green Party of St. Louis, MO, May 31, 2013, http://www.gateway-greens.org/content/march-against-monsanto-worldwide-event-makes-history

3. Anomaly, "Two million protesters attend 'March Against Monsanto' in 436 cities in 52 countries," *FreakOutNation*, May 26, 2013, http://freakoutnation.com/2013/05/26/two-million-protesters-attend-march-against-monsanto-in-436-cities-in-52-countries/

4. Elizabeth Renter, "Europe, Nations Around The World Rejecting Monsanto," *Philosophers Stone*, June 5, 2013,

http://philosophers-stone.co.uk/wordpress/2013/06/europe-nations-around-the-world-rejecting-monsanto/

5. "Bullsh*t walks, and it carries an anti-Monsanto sign," *Bad Skeptic*, May 25, 2013, http://badskeptic.com/?p=490

6. "UK Organisations Challenge Basis for GM Wheat Trials," *Sustainable Pulse*, June 3, 2013, http://sustainablepulse.com/2013/06/03/uk-organizations-challenge-basis-for-gm-wheat-trials/

7. "Washington farmers sue Monsanto over GMO wheat," *King Broadcasting Company*, June 7, 2013, http://www.king5.com/news/local/Washington-farmers-sue-Monsanto-over-GMO-wheat-210563651.html

8. Jacob Chamberlain, "Scientists Find Holes in Monsanto GM Wheat Denial, *Common Dreams*, June 6, 2013, https://www.commondreams.org/headline/2013/06/06-1

9. Shannon Dininny, Associated Press, "Farmers sue Monsanto over genetically modified wheat," *Komo News Network*, June 6, 2013, http://www.komonews.com/news/local/Wash-farmers-sue-Monsanto-over-GMO-wheat-210460121.html

10. "Stephen Colbert On Monsanto: GMO Wheat Is 'The Return Of The Walking Bread'," *The Huffington Post*, June 6, 2013, http://www.huffingtonpost.com/2013/06/06/stephen-colbert-monsanto-gmo-seeds-wheat_n_3399249.html

11. "Massive Database of GMO Evidence gives Worldwide Picture of Harm," *Sustainable Pulse*, June 7, 2013, http://sustainablepulse.com/2013/06/07/massive-database-of-gmo-evidence-gives-worldwide-picture-of-harm/

12. "Connecticut Celebrates GMO Labeling Victory," *Sustainable Pulse*, June 4, 2013, http://sustainablepulse.com/2013/06/04/connecticut-celebrates-gmo-labeling-victory/

13. "DSM-IV and DSM-5 Criteria for the Personality Disorders," *American Psychiatric Association*, 2012,

http://www.psi.uba.ar/academica/carrerasdegrado/psicologia/sitio
s_catedras/practicas_profesionales/610_clinica_cuadrosfront_psic
osis/material/dsm.pdf

Lie #28: Monsanto is Transparent

1. "Our Pledge," *Monsanto*, p. v,
http://www.monsanto.com/SiteCollectionDocuments/Code-of-
Business-Conduct-PDFs/code_of_conduct_english.pdf

2. Nils, Mulvad, "GMO lose Europe – victory for environmental
organizations," *Investigative Reporting Denmark*," May 29, 2013,
http://www.ir-d.dk/gmo-lose-europe-victory-for-environmental-
organisations/

3. "Rammed down our throats," *noseweek*, September, 2005,
http://www.responsibletechnology.org/docs/94.pdf

4. "Activist Investor to Challenge Monsanto CEO to be More
Transparent at January 31 Annual Shareholder Meeting," *Occupy
Monsanto*, January 30, 2013, http://occupy-
monsanto.com/tag/proposition-37/

Lie #29: GM Wheat Poses No Concern

1. "Monsanto and GM Wheat, Dr. Robb Fraley Discusses GM Wheat
(video)," *Monsanto*,
http://www.monsanto.com/gmwheat/Pages/default.aspx

2. "Monsanto sued over discovery of GM wheat sprouts,"
Minnesota Farm Guide, June 10, 2013,
http://www.minnesotafarmguide.com/news/regional/monsanto-
sued-over-discovery-of-gm-wheat-sprouts/article_c3ea1168-d1e0-
11e2-8071-001a4bcf887a.html

3. David Knowles, "Monsanto says sabotage may be behind GMO
wheat in Oregon as more farmers file suit," *New York Daily News*,
June 6, 2013,
http://www.nydailynews.com/news/national/monsanto-sabotage-
behind-oregon-gmo-wheat-article-1.1365598

4. "Monsanto Legal Risks Linger With Suit as Wheat Futures
Rebound," *AgWeb*,
http://www.agweb.com/mobile/newsdetail.aspx?ArticleId=336468

5. Fritz Kreiss, "Monsanto Found to Have 2 'Secret' GMO Wheat Test Fields in the US at this Time," *Occupy Monsanto*, June 4, 2013, http://occupymonsanto360.org/blog/monsanto-found-to-have-2-secret-gmo-wheat-test-fields-in-the-us-at-this-time/

6. Sean Ellis, "Monsanto creating new Wheat Technology Center in Idaho," *Capital Press*, June 6, 2013, http://www.capitalpress.com/content/SE-Monsanto-Idaho-Main-061413

7. Amanda Taylor, "Monsanto: The Big Bad Wolf," *The Vancouver Vector*, April 11th, 2013, http://www.vancouvervector.com/world/monsanto-the-big-bad-wolf/

Lie #30: GMO Labels Would Only Confuse You

1. "TAKING A STAND: PROPOSITION 37, THE CALIFORNIA LABELING PROPOSAL," *Monsanto*, http://monsantoblog.com/2012/08/14/taking-a-stand-proposition-37-the-california-labeling-proposal/

2. "Broad Coalition Opposes Legislation to Require GE Labeling," *Biotechnology Industry Association*, May 9, 2013,

http://www.bio.org/advocacy/letters/broad-coalition-opposes-legislation-require-ge-labeling

3. "Whole Foods Market GMO Labeling Announcement Reverberating Through Industry," *Institute For Responsible Technology*, http://www.responsibletechnology.org/posts/whole-foods-market-gmo-labeling-announcement-reverberating-through-industry/

4. Ocean Robbins, "Did Monsanto Trick California Voters?" *Huffington Post,* http://www.huffingtonpost.com/ocean-robbins/monsanto-prop-37_b_2088934.html

5. *Just Label It!,* http://justlabelit.org/

6. "Battle Brewing Over Labeling of Genetically Modified Food," *New York Times*,

http://www.nytimes.com/2012/05/25/science/dispute-over-labeling-of-genetically-modified-food.html?_r=0

Lie #31: Almost All Foods Are Genetically Modified

1. "How Are We Doing It?" *Monsanto*, http://www.monsanto.com/improvingagriculture/Pages/modern-breeding-techniques.aspx

2. "How Are We Doing It? Biotechnology 101," *Monsanto*, http://www.monsanto.com/improvingagriculture/Pages/biotechnology-101.aspx

3. "What Is A GMO?" *Amandala Newspaper*, March 1, 2013, http://amandala.com.bz/news/gmo-awareness-month-week-1-gmo/

4. "Glyphosate Factsheet," *Mindfully.org*, http://www.mindfully.org/Pesticide/Roundup-Glyphosate-Factsheet-Cox.htm

5. "Blamed for Bee Collapse, Monsanto Buys Leading Bee Research Firm," *Natural Society*, http://naturalsociety.com/monsanto-bee-collapse-buys-bee-research-firm/

6. Brower, L., et al., "Decline of monarch butterflies overwintering in Mexico: is the migratory phenomenon at risk?" *Insect Conservation and Diversity* Volume 5, Issue 2 (March 2012): pp. 95-100. "Three factors are implicated in the downward trend in the monarch's abundance: (i) the loss of and reduction in quality of critical overwintering habitat in Mexico through extensive illegal logging; (ii) the widespread reduction of breeding habitat in the United States due to continuing land development and the killing of the monarch's principal larval foodplant, the common milkweed Asclepias syriaca L. (Asclepiadaceae), because of increased use of glyphosate herbicide to kill weeds growing in genetically engineered, herbicide-resistant crops; and (iii) periodic extreme weather conditions, such as those that occurred most recently in 2009, that decrease both the spring breeding in Texas and the subsequent spring and summer breeding generations in the eastern USA and southern Canada.

7. Michael Antoniou, Claire Robinson, John Fagan, GMO Myths and

Truths: An evidence-based examination of the claims made for the safety and efficacy of genetically modified crops, *Earth Open Source*, June 2012, p. 9, http://www.nongmoproject.org/wp-content/uploads/2010/08/GMO_Myths_and_Truths_1.31.pdf

8. "GMO Dangers," *Institute For Responsible Technology*, http://www.responsibletechnology.org/gmo-dangers

9. "Leadership," *Center For Food Safety*, http://www.centerforfoodsafety.org/staff

10. Food Revolution Summit, https://www.facebook.com/foodrevolutionsummit, https://www.facebook.com/photo.php?fbid=463693837039482&set=a.3 99871986755001.92382.282915761783958&type=1&theater

Lie #32: The FDA Said Prop 37 Would Mislead People

1. Statement printed on No on 37 mailer, http://kpbs.media.clients.ellingtoncms.com/news/documents/201 2/10/19/NO_flyer.pdf

2. Claire Trageser, "Supporters Of GMO Labeling Call 'No On 37' Campaign Mailers 'Criminal'," *KPBS Public Broadcasting*, Friday, October 19, 2012, http://www.kpbs.org/news/2012/oct/19/supporters-prop-37-call-nos-campaign-mailers-gmo/

3. "RPT-California GMO measure may fail after food industry fights back," *Reuters*, http://www.reuters.com/article/2012/11/05/california-gmo-idUSL1E8M2DGD20121105

Lie #33: Labeling Initiatives Require Scary Warnings on GM Foods

1. "TAKING A STAND: PROPOSITION 37, THE CALIFORNIA LABELING PROPOSAL," *Monsanto*, http://monsantoblog.com/2012/08/14/taking-a-stand-proposition-37-the-california-labeling-proposal/

2. Brad Shannon, "GMO battle lands in Washington," *The Olympian*, July 14, 2013,

http://www.theolympian.com/2013/07/14/2621095/gmo-battle-lands-in-washington.html

3. Michele Simon, "Top 10 Lies Told by Monsanto on GMO Labeling in California," *The Huffington Post*, August 22, 2012, http://www.huffingtonpost.com/michele-simon/top-10-lies-told-by-monsa_b_1819731.html

4. Ronnie Cummins, "Millions Against Monsanto: The Food Fight of Our Lives," *AlterNet*, April 13, 2012, http://truth-out.org/news/item/8501-millions-against-monsanto-the-food-fight-of-our-lives "'If you put a label on genetically engineered food you might as well put a skull and crossbones on it.' -- Norman Braksick, president of Asgrow Seed Co., a subsidiary of Monsanto, quoted in the Kansas City Star, March 7, 1994"

Lie #34: Stanford University Employs Henry Miller

1. "TV ad against food labeling initiative Proposition 37 is pulled," *Los Angeles Times*, http://articles.latimes.com/2012/oct/04/business/la-fi-mo-anti-proposition-37-ad-pulled-20121004

Lie #35: GMO Labels Will Limit Choice

1. "TAKING A STAND: PROPOSITION 37, THE CALIFORNIA LABELING PROPOSAL," *Monsanto*, http://monsantoblog.com/2012/08/14/taking-a-stand-proposition-37-the-california-labeling-proposal/

2. Michele Simon, "Top 10 Lies Told by Monsanto on GMO Labeling in California," *The Huffington Post*, August 22, 2012, http://www.huffingtonpost.com/michele-simon/top-10-lies-told-by-monsa_b_1819731.html

3. "Are the 'Traitor Brand' Parents Hiding Behind the GMA?" *Organic Consumers Association*, http://www.organicconsumers.org/bytes/ob384.html

4. Scientific American Editorial Board, "Labels for GMO Foods Are a Bad Idea," NO on 522, August 20, 2013, http://www.votenoon522.com/labels-for-gmo-foods-are-a-bad-idea/

Lie #36: People in Favor Of GMO Labels Oppose Medicine and Science

1. "Why Health & Medical Experts Oppose the Flawed Food Labeling Proposition," NoProp37.com, http://www.noprop37.com/files/No-on-37-HEALTH-GROUPS-OPPOSE-FACT-SHEET.pdf

2. "Yes on Prop 37 Endorsements," *carighttoknow.org*, http://www.carighttoknow.org/endorsements

Lie #37: The Main Proponents of GMO Labels Are Special Interest Groups

1. "TAKING A STAND: PROPOSITION 37, THE CALIFORNIA LABELING PROPOSAL," *Monsanto*, http://monsantoblog.com/2012/08/14/taking-a-stand-proposition-37-the-california-labeling-proposal/

2. "Yes on Prop 37 Endorsements," *carighttoknow.org*, http://www.carighttoknow.org/endorsements

Lie #38: GMO Labels Increase Costs

1. "FACTS ABOUT I-522: It's not what it seems to be…," *NO on 522*,http://factsabout522.com/

2. "Association of Washington Business opposes Initiative 522," *Port Orchard Independent*, May 14, 2013, http://www.portorchardindependent.com/news/207246511.html

3. Jason Hoppin, "In Prop 37 food fight, is fair play losing out?" *Santa Cruz Sentinel*, September 30, 2012, http://www.santacruzsentinel.com/localnews/ci_21667896/prop-37-food-fight-is-fair-play-losing

4. John Robbins, "John Robbins at The Longevity Now Conference May 2013," *The Longevity Now Conference*, May 2013, http://www.thelongevitynowconference.com/free-bonus-vids.php

5. Zack Kaldveer and Ronnie Cummins, "The Biotech Industry Has Trotted Out a Flimsy Lie to Avoid Labeling the Food We Buy as Genetically Modified," *AlterNet*, April 15, 2013,

http://www.alternet.org/food/biotech-industry-has-trotted-out-flimsy-lie-avoid-labeling-food-we-buy-genetically-modified

6. "Activist Investor to Challenge Monsanto CEO to be More Transparent at January 31 Annual Shareholder Meeting," *Occupy Monsanto*, January 31, 2013, http://occupy-monsanto.com/press-release-for-the-monsanto-annual-shareholder-meeting/

Lie #39: Biotech Food Safety Is Not Monsanto's Responsibility

1. Michael Pollen, "Playing God in the Garden," *New York Times Magazine on GE Crops, The New York Times Sunday Magazine*, October 25, 1998,
http://www.organicconsumers.org/ge/playinggd.htm

2. "How We Establish Biotech Crop Safety: Product Characterization," *Monsanto*,
http://www.monsanto.com/newsviews/Pages/Biotech-Crop-Safety-Product-Characterization.aspx

3. FDA Letter, Letter from Alan M. Rulis, Office of Premarket Approval, Center for Food Safety and Applied Nutrition, FDA to Dr. Kent Croon, Regulatory Affairs Manager, Monsanto Company, Sept 25, 1996, http://www.responsibletechnology.org/fraud/faulty-regulations/An-FDA-Created-Health-Crisis-Circles-the-Globe-October-2007#_edn14

Lie #40: Agent Orange Does Not Cause Serious Health Effects

1. "Agent Orange Victims Sue Monsanto," *CorpWatch*,
http://www.corpwatch.org/article.php?id=11638

2. "The Quest for Additional Relief," *Agent Orange Record*,
http://www.agentorangerecord.com/information/the_quest_for_additional_relief/

3. "Monsanto, Agent Orange, Dioxins and Plan Columbia," *SourceWatch*,
http://sourcewatch.org/index.php?title=Monsanto,_Agent_Orange,_Dioxins_and_Plan_Columbia

4. Marie-Monique Robin, "The World According To Monsanto: Pollution, Corruption, and the Control of Our Food Supply, an Investigation into the World's Most Controversial Company," The New Press, New York, 2010, pp. 48-51

5. "Reported Illnesses," *Agent Orange Legacy*, http://agentorangelegacy.com/reported-illnesses/

The complete list includes 493 illnesses suspected to be caused by Agent Orange.

6. "Agent Orange: Background on Monsanto's Involvement," *Monsanto*, http://www.monsanto.com/newsviews/Pages/agent-orange-background-monsanto-involvement.aspx

See also:

Images of Agent Orange Victims, https://www.google.com/search?q=agent+orange+images&hl=en&safe=off&source=lnms&tbm=isch&sa=X&ei=X-hFUdNzxMWtAZq3gaAB&ved=0CAoQ_AUoAQ&biw=1127&bih=670

"Agent Orange – Vietnam," *ABC Australia*, http://www.youtube.com/watch?v=GJxb7CY13uc

"Health effects of Agent Orange/Dioxin," *War Legacies Project*, http://www.warlegacies.org/health.htm

Lie #41: No Need to Test for Safety of GM Foods in Humans

1. "Food Safety," *Monsanto*, http://www.monsanto.com/newsviews/Pages/food-safety.aspx

2. "The Importance of Safety," *Monsanto*, http://www.monsanto.com/improvingagriculture/Pages/the-importance-of-safety.aspx

3. "Biotech Propaganda Cooks Dangers out of GM Potatoes," *Institute For Responsible Technology*, http://www.responsibletechnology.org/posts/biotech-propaganda-cooks-dangers-out-of-gm-potatoes-2/

4. Jeffrey M. Smith, *Genetic Roulette: The Documented Health Risks of Genetically Engineered Foods*, Yes! Books, Fairfield, IA, 2007, p. 22

5. Jeffrey M. Smith, *Seeds of Deception: Exposing Industry and Government Lies About the Safety of the Genetically Engineered Foods You're Eating*, Yes! Books, Fairfield, Iowa, 2003, p. 9

6. *GMOEvidence.com*, www.gmoevidence.com

7. "Biotech's Dirty Tricks Exposed in New Documentary Scientists Under Attack," *Institute For Responsible Technology*, http://www.responsibletechnology.org/posts/biotech's-dirty-tricks-exposed-in-new-documentary-scientists-under-attack/

8. "Critics Answered," *GMOSeralini*, http://gmoseralini.org/category/critics-answered/

9. John Vidal, "FSA 'endangering public health' by ignoring concerns over GM food,' *The Guardian*, September 6, 2013, http://gmoseralini.org/fsa-endangering-public-health-by-ignoring-concerns-over-gm-food/

10. Shicana Allen, "This little piggy was fed GMOs," *The Bulletin*, http://thebulletin.ca/this-little-piggy-was-fed-gmos/

11. "65 Health Risks of GM Foods," *Institute for Responsible Technology*, http://www.responsibletechnology.org/gmo-dangers/65-health-risks/1notes

12. "GM Health Risks Week: Speaking Tour 2nd-8th September: This week UK citizens have an opportunity to find out more about the risks posed by GMOs in the food chain, hear expert evidence and challenge the UK government........," *Ecologist*, September 2, 2013, http://www.theecologist.org/calendar/2065052/gm_health_risks_week_speaking_tour_2nd8th_september.html

Lie #42: Monsanto is A New Company

1. "A New Pledge for a New Company," Remarks by Hendrik A. Verfaillie, President and Chief Executive Officer, Monsanto Company, Farm Journal Conference, Washington, D.C., November 27, 2000, http://www.biotech-info.net/new_Monsanto.html

2. Cynthia A. Diaz-Shephard, "NYC Council Members Introduce PCB Bill," *NewsInferno*, May 13, 2011, http://www.newsinferno.com/?p=31123

3. "Solutia Settles Environmental Claims With Monsanto (Update3)," *Bloomburg*, August 16, 2007, http://www.bloomberg.com/apps/news?pid=newsarchive&sid=agr SpS_FQWHQ&refer=home

4. Wayne Barrett, "Mitt Romney, Monsanto Man," *The Nation*, September 12, 2012, http://www.thenation.com/article/169885/mitt-romney-monsanto-man#

5. "Korean Supreme Court Reverses and Remands Agent Orange Judgment," Monsanto, July 12, 2013, http://www.monsanto.com/newsviews/Pages/korean-supreme-court-reverses-and-remands-agent-orange-judgment.aspx

Lie #43: Biotechnology Increases Crop Yields

1. "A New Pledge for a New Company," Remarks by Hendrik A. Verfaillie, President and Chief Executive Officer, Monsanto Company, Farm Journal Conference, Washington, D.C., November 27, 2000 http://www.biotech-info.net/new_Monsanto.html

2. "A SCIENCE PIONEER'S JOURNEY IN AGRICULTURE," *monsantoblog.com*, June 19, 2013, http://monsantoblog.com/2013/06/19/a-science-pioneers-journey-in-agriculture/

3. Jeffrey Smith, "The Big GMO Cover-Up," Institute For Responsible Technology, November 6, 2009, http://www.responsibletechnology.org/gmo-coverup

4. "University of Canterbury Researchers: GM is a Failing Biotechnology," *Sustainable Pulse*, June 20, 2013, http://sustainablepulse.com/2013/06/20/university-of-canterbury-researchers-gm-is-a-failing-biotechnology/

5. "Analysis Finds Monsanto's GE Corn Nutritionally Inferior and High in Toxins," *Mercola.com*, April 30, 2013, http://articles.mercola.com/sites/articles/archive/2013/04/30/mo nsanto-gmo-corn.aspx

6. "How Does Roundup Work?" *BizPro eSources*,

http://bizpro.horizononline.com/assets/files/Horizon_HowDoesRoundupWork.pdf

7. "Monsanto's Roundup Triggers Over 40 Plant Diseases and Endangers Human and Animal Health," *Institute For Responsible Technology*, http://www.responsibletechnology.org/posts/monsanto's-roundup-triggers-over-40-plant-diseases/

Lie #44: Romney Has No Favors to Repay

1. "Mitt Romney & the Monsanto connection," *YouTube*, July 9, 2012, http://www.youtube.com/watch?v=s6VnpfxBqCw

2. Aviva Shen, "Romney And Bain Boosted Agriculture Giant Monsanto In Spite Of Toxic Past," *ThinkProgress*, September 14, 2012, http://thinkprogress.org/election/2012/09/14/850321/romney-monsanto/?mobile=nc

3. Wayne Barrett, "Mitt Romney, Monsanto Man, *The Nation*, September 12, 2012, http://www.thenation.com/article/169885/mitt-romney-monsanto-man#

4. "No Matter Who Wins the 2012 Presidential Election Monsanto Benefits," *The Progressive Cynic*, November 5, 2012, http://theprogressivecynic.com/2012/11/05/no-matter-who-wins-the-2012-presidential-election-monsanto-benefits/

Lie #45: Obama Will Label GMOs

1. "Obama signs Monsanto Protection Act! Betrays America - It's Time to Label GMOs!" *Food Democracy Now*, March 27, 2013, http://www.fooddemocracynow.org/blog/2013/mar/27/obama_signs_monsanto_protection_act/

2. "You're Appointing Who? Please Obama, Say It's Not So!" *The Institute For Responsible Technology*, July 23, 2009, http://www.responsibletechnology.org/posts/youre-appointing-who-please-obama-say-its-not-so/

3. "Obama's Team Includes Dangerous Biotech 'Yes Men'," *The Institute For Responsible Technology*,

http://www.responsibletechnology.org/posts/obamas-team-includes-dangerous-biotech-yes-men/

4. Barbara Minton, "Obama or Romney? Find Out What They Think of You," *AlignLife*, October 26, 2012,
http://alignlife.com/articles/food/obama-or-romney-both-eat-organic-while-promoting-gmos-for-us/

5. Robbie Hanna Anderman, "Obama's Deregulation of GMO Crops," *Tikkun*, May 27, 2011,
http://www.tikkun.org/nextgen/obamas-deregulation-of-gmo-crops

6. "National Bioeconomy Blueprint," *The White House*, April 2012,
http://www.whitehouse.gov/sites/default/files/microsites/ostp/national_bioeconomy_blueprint_april_2012.pdf

Lie #46: Monsanto Participates Constructively in Politics

1. "Political Disclosures," *Monsanto*,
http://www.monsanto.com/whoweare/Pages/political-disclosures.aspx

2. Ted Nace, *Gangs of America: The Rise of Corporate Power and the Disabling of Democracy (Bk Currents)*, Berrett-Koehler Publishers, Inc., San Francisco, CA, 2003.
http://www.amazon.com/Gangs-America-Corporate-Disabling-Democracy/dp/1576753190/

3. Barbara Minton, "Obama or Romney? Find Out What They Think of You," *AlignLife*, October 26, 2012,
http://alignlife.com/articles/food/obama-or-romney-both-eat-organic-while-promoting-gmos-for-us/

4. "Ed Griffin on the Left / Right Paradigm (Recommended)," *YouTube*, http://www.youtube.com/watch?v=rxDwT55rmIw

5. "United States of Monsanto: GMO Giant is Now Litigation Proof," *RTAmerica*, March 29, 2013,
http://www.youtube.com/watch?v=E5lkiTnI9V0

Lie #47: Giving Is Natural For Monsanto

1. "Corporate Giving," *Monsanto*,

http://www.monsanto.com/whoweare/Pages/corporate-giving.aspx

2. Kamalakar Duvvuru, "Monsanto and Its Philanthropy," *Dissident Voice*, May 2, 2009, http://dissidentvoice.org/2009/05/monsanto-and-its-philanthropy/ Statement made by Hugh Grant, Chairman, President, and CEO of Monsanto

3. Matilda Lee, "Monsanto, Bayer and Dow face trial for 'systematic human rights abuses'," *The Ecologist*, November 16, 2011, http://www.theecologist.org/News/news_analysis/1122020/mons anto_bayer_and_dow_face_trial_for_systematic_human_rights_ab uses.html

4. "Gene Giants Seek 'Philanthrogopoly'," *ETC Group*, March 7, 2013,

http://www.etcgroup.org/content/gene-giants-seek-philanthrogopoly

5. Beverly Bell, "Haitian Farmers Commit to Burning Monsanto Hybrid Seeds," *The Huffington Post*, May 17, 2010, http://www.huffingtonpost.com/beverly-bell/haitian-farmers-commit-to_b_578807.html

6. Daniel Klein, "Perennial Plate in India: GMOs and Farmer Suicides [VIDEO]," *Civil Eats*, February 19, 2013, http://civileats.com/2013/02/19/perennial-plate-in-india-gmos-and-farmer-suicides/

7. "Our Mission," *Monsanto Fund*, http://www.monsantofund.org/about/our-mission/

Lie #48: Monsanto Values Doing Things the Right Way

1. "Code of Business Conduct,", *Monsanto*, p. 1, http://www.monsanto.com/SiteCollectionDocuments/Code-of-Business-Conduct-PDFs/code_of_conduct_english.pdf

2. Marie-Monique Robin, *The World According To Monsanto: Pollution, Corruption, and the Control of Our Food Supply, an Investigation into the World's Most Controversial Company*, The New Press, New York, 2010, http://www.amazon.com/World-According-Monsanto-Marie-Monique-Robin/dp/1595587098/

3. Jeffrey M. Smith, *Seeds of Deception: Exposing Industry and Government Lies About the Safety of the Genetically Engineered Foods You're Eating*, Yes! Books, Fairfield, Iowa, 2003, http://www.amazon.com/Seeds-Deception-Government-Genetically-Engineered/dp/0972966587/

4. William F. Engdahl, *Seeds of Destruction: The Hidden Agenda of Genetic Manipulation*, Global Research, Montreal, Quebec, Canada, 2007, http://www.amazon.com/Seeds-Destruction-Hidden-Genetic-Manipulation/dp/0973714727/

Lie #49: Monsanto Is Committed to Sustainable Agriculture

1. "Our Commitment to Sustainable Agriculture," *Monsanto*, http://www.monsanto.com/whoweare/Pages/our-commitment-to-sustainable-agriculture.aspx

2. "SiteMap," *Monsanto*, http://www.monsanto.com/Pages/sitemap.aspx

3. Dr. Mercola, "How Organic Farming Could Release Us From the Curse of Fertilizer," *Mercola.com*, July 2, 2013, http://articles.mercola.com/sites/articles/archive/2013/07/02/fertilizer.aspx

4. Tom Philpott, "Are We Heading Toward Peak Fertilizer?" *Mother Jones*, November 28, 2012, http://www.motherjones.com/tom-philpott/2012/11/are-we-heading-toward-peak-fertilizer

5. Frances Moore Lappé and Anna Lappé, "Choice of Monsanto Betrays World Food Prize Purpose, Say Global Leaders," *The Huffington Post*, June 26, 2013, http://www.huffingtonpost.com/frances-moore-lappe-and-anna-lappe/choice-of-monsanto-betray_b_3499045.html

6. "Two Options," (Video), *Navdanya*, http://seedfreedom.in/

See also:

"Anna Lappé & Food MythBusters -- Do we really need industrial agriculture to feed the world? (video)" *RealFoodMediaProject*, http://www.youtube.com/watch?feature=player_embedded&v=uem2ceZMxYk

Lie #50: You Can Trust Monsanto

1. "Playing God in the Garden, New York Times Magazine on GE Crops, *The New York Times Sunday Magazine*, (October 25, 1998), http://www.organicconsumers.org/ge/playinggd.htm

Conclusion

1. "Rammed down our throats," *noseweek*, September, 2005, http://www.responsibletechnology.org/docs/94.pdf

About the Author

Brett Wilcox grew up in suburban USA on three quarters of an acre where he enjoyed eating fresh fruits and vegetables from the family garden. He is a Licensed Professional Counselor, an award-winning author, and has a keen interest in health and well-being.

He and his teen-aged son, David, are preparing to run across the U.S.A. in 2014. If successful, David will be the youngest runner and the running duo will be the first father/son team to complete this run. Brett's wife, Kris, and daughter, Olivia, will crew for the runners. They welcome opportunities to speak to the public and to the media about their run, and to share their passion for a safe, healthy, and natural food supply.

Take part in their journey at RunningTheCountry.com or join the Facebook group Running the Country. Tax-deductible donations are gratefully accepted. They are running the country to stop Monsanto from running the country.

Seed Freedom Now!

Author's Note

Unlike Monsanto, the people employed by Monsanto are indeed humans. They want their children to grow up in a safe, clean, and healthy world just as you and I do. May they work diligently to reform Monsanto from within the company, and may we work together for the betterment of the earth, her creations, and our children.